FIVE SEASONS *of* OBSESSION

FIVE
SEASONS
of OBSESSION

New & Selected Poems

Ned O'Gorman

BOOKS & CO.
A Turtle Point Press Imprint
NEW YORK

BOOKS & CO.
Turtle Point Press
New York

© *2001 by Ned O'Gorman*

Some of these poems
have previously appeared in
The New Yorker, Partisan Review,
Harpers Bazaar, Commonweal,
The Catholic Worker, The Paris Review,
The Beloit Poetry Journal, Poetry,
Argestes, The Chattahoochee Review,
and The Larcome Review.

PUBLISHER'S CATALOGING-IN-PUBLICATION
O'Gorman, Ned, 1929–
Five seasons of obsession : new & selected poems /
Ned O'Gorman. — 1st ed.
p. cm.
ISBN 1-885586-55-8
1. Nature—Poetry.   2. Love—Poetry.
3. Faith—Poetry.   I. Title.
PS3565.G6F58 2001   811'.5'4
QBI01-700262

LCCN 2001 131204

Design and composition by Melissa Ehn at
Wilsted & Taylor Publishing Services

This book is for my teachers—

Lincoln Kirstein

Sir Isaiah Berlin

Dame Janet Baker

Peter Worsley

Dorothea Straus

and

Jane Howe

CONTENTS

from *How to Put Out a Fire* (1984)

New Poems

A FEW WORDS ON NED O'GORMAN'S NEW & SELECTED POEMS

by Ned Rorem

We share the same Manhattan zip code. I used to wonder if the area were large enough to contain two such Neds. But we complement each other. He is outward and rugged, if not too self-revealing; I'm effete and neurotic and a bit self-pitying. And I'm transparent, while he's dense—and sometimes hard to understand.

Yet is art ever understood, rather than felt? Can music be proven to mean anything? Can poetry (any poetry, from Mother Goose to T. S. Eliot) be scanned so as to have the same literal significance for all readers? Art, like love—or hate—is intuited rather than parsed. And since opposites attract, I'm drawn to Ned O'Gorman, even as he says he is to me.

One can experience his verse as one experiences the loss of virginity, or the finding of a 100-dollar bill on a park bench. He tells us what we did not know we know. Look, for example, at the novel but unforced rhymes and images in *Winter*:

> The matter of intellect is arctic.
> . . . and the reign
> of intellect collapses on petrified oceans of snow.

Or the carnality of *Vegetable-Life*:

> Where the pulp lifts its germ and the sludge of beauty lies.

Or the fright—yes, the fright—in *A Rectification of the Lyric*:

> There is
> nothing left at all, anywhere.
> Place has ceased to be . . .
> . . . time is broken in the corner
> of the eye.

Or his take on love in *A Philosophy*:

> . . . Love is not easy and likely to trouble dreams.
> . . . It is man's way of life . . .
> until the end of love; until the body's end.

Or his unwitting reuniting of old acquaintances in *Fulco di Verdura: A Vanity*. I knew and liked Fulco a half-century ago, and lost him, then found him again in Ned's poem. Likewise I found my alcoholism of yore in *Drunk on the Lord's Wine*, but now it's turned into faith.

Peace, After Long Madness, echoing Yeats's rhythms, as *Panther* echoes Cavafy's, is a boon to any insomniac. *Ram* is sheer sex, and so in a way is *Dreams Erotic, Dreams Not*. I could go on for pages.

For I deeply need Ned's poetry. Like his name, it is part of my life.

—15 January 2001

from

The Night
of the Hammer

1959

The Aunt

When children are very young
aunts can be quite anyone
who is old and unremarkable.
This aunt was archetypically correct,

doubting children and their dogs,
aching when it rained, praying for accord
between the sexes and the late arrival.
Content with nothing if it were right. . . .

When I was young I thought of God
as color and found that it was hard
to banish him to blue or white,
the colors I knew from watching.

Once when I was ill and wrapped in bed,
at five o'clock my Aunt stood at my head
and swished me with her crinkled hand.
And, as she bent to kiss me, I saw descending

an assault of color, moving in the air,
a troop of peacocks' tails, a flair
of spectrum wrenched from light.
Astounded with this sudden firework

I carefully constructed God again,
his temper and his mind, his ken,
his fatal hand, and discovered
my Aunt had carried on her head

My God without a single angel
to help her with the load.
                          When will
the Aunt reveal again the answer and
the question: *Quem colorem habet Sapientia?*

The Swing

Once in the air I'll not come down
until my eyes are cleared of
sound and filled with sights
I have not touched and stones I
have not found. Enemies
cannot reveal the food of love
nor lovers how the kiss should be
but in the air I'll play
battue with lights, receive
the serpent with my foot
and understand for all I've
learned why Thales died
(if all were water) why trees
burn down (if all is flame)
and why when stars shine in my
room I hear the theory of pain.
I shall swing, swing beyond
myself to rock with every hurt
of wind and slumber in the coming
down in speed of light and graphs of stone.

A Description of the Sea for Lena Lenzi Who Has Never Seen It

There is no reason in it.
It is known by extravagance.
Think how the water falls
over the hill when you tip
a copper dish after washing.
The descent is torrential
like unfolding a sheet
in the sun. A residential
sea made from the tasks
of a Tuscan day. That's
the sea, a morning's wifery.

There's a green light in it.
Think of the branches
of those umbrella pines
that catch green beneath them
as a cardinal crowds
all scarlet on his head.
Or a salamander lost
in thoughts of furnaces and flints
waits among the honeysuckle
where bees, hammers in their wings,
build pontoons across seas of lights.

There's the noise of the noon
bus in it, like a swoon
of girls hollering with rage
that Tom, decrepit cat, had

chewed their darling captive
in its cage. Or a fix of soldiers
pale from urging priests from sleep
and saints from pinnacles
rail on a hill and rock the air
with cannon. That's the sea,
my simile of the mind's famine.

There's the black of night in it.
Watch the valley from Vespucci's
tower when the Arno cracks the ark
of heaven and the pines pull
together like a line of quail
who sight the barrel through
the bush. The moon turns
the furrows of the sea
and alters then the scape and
the span of it, in imitation
of these black and natural things.

The sun glares through light
like a girl following a wasp
down her first communion veil;
or oxen touching fire with
their red pompons. It's the rain
of every spring since partisans
lost among the poppies closed
their eyes to dream the Tiber
from their tears. In the building
of an April night the world
contrives its salts and ambergris.

The sea's the world's hot fiber,
the caterwauling cosmology

of the brainless love of God.
The sea is the lexicon of
gardens and the weight of winds.
It has no sweetness of streams
nor has it any bottomside like
pools. The sea's a net of water,
a prairie of sunken barge and
sides of mountains only climbed
by fish. I tell you, travel to it!

The Kiss

Talk of passion is a winter thing,
a huddle of girls descending wind.
There is no vehicle in a kiss
to carry fury and originality.
In that wherewithal of mouth
the body greets with cannon
the profundis and halt clamavi
of the virgin. Dying is a kiss,
it has broken me. It rimes with tiger
and the gallow tree.

Agamemnon as Arcady

I.

In forms of dark, in single attack,
the pheasants rose into the trees
at five. I think they sprang
from caverns in the earth
so suddenly they appeared,
so fast their rising up.

The sounds of doom are various.
With a sound that pine boughs make
when loosed from snow they spring back
into symmetry the pheasants toppled
from their trees, as if my bell
was a fowler's horn, and fell to Dis
through windows at my feet.

I thought of kites and cannibals,
and Agamemnon in his armored barge.

II.

In fields of lemon trees
I dreamed of Agamemnon,
of tombs, of low pitched horns.
Bees were nuncios to the Trojan
dawn where Assassination sniffed the air
computing sweetness with its canine snout.

Black Angus sunned like caliphs
on the grass; ducks kicked
hex on the dazzling stream.

It's dynasties that shift the time
and I remembered Agamemnon stuttering
toward regalia.

An Art of Poetry

The advantage of the line is direction
to the generate point
where torrid with gesture
it swerves upon itself
and builds the primitive arc,
deranged center, wrought circle.
For Euclid and an Arabian child
shape is not gainsaid
nor left pillared to a gathering of
inch, but must in its mode, category,
in the spring of its architecture
move fast to hoop.

II.

When rhetoric begins poetry does.
In the disputation of the will
the voyages took by the eye.
In its handlings of horns
the ear will utter a lesson:
the singing of seas,
growling gulls.
When the corn in gold turrets
burns in the sun's punctual fire.
The scuffle of the scorpion
across the winter web.

Poetry begins where rhetoric does.
When poetry speaks
a theater lamentation, when it seems
Lear did mightily by the hurricane.

III.

I've told you again and again
how the world began.
                        How the
elephant grew, that fish learned
the sea was best, why apes walked,
How calamity befell Eve.
How Jehovah watched like a club-footed
girl stalking a swan.
                        I've told you
that the middle-of-words are fixed
to a kite and are reachless;
though alternate and charged
the poles are still, that color
melted in flame yields nothing.

With a slow voice I've told
you love betters love, that alphabet
is Adam trying his ribs for woman.

I've told you the history of my history,
the wild Arabia of my brow, your map
to reconnoiter as you will, teeming
with the uncalamity of your boyhood.

Two Homilies

For Mark Van Doren

I.

Expect this,
that rock may be supposéd bear
or any elephant may shiver
from a rose
and some undoubted seer
may hold the brainless edge of thought.
O anything may be a circle
or any man, however hump
may move like cleanest prince
through ordinary halls and
touch each foot on hunted gold.
That dark imago of a bird
may be a nun who rises
to some accident of trumpet
that merely is
a falling red balloon.
O beautiful collision
where mind meets the shaping light
and waits in adoration
while all things clang.

II.

It may or may not be decisive
whether or not the sun is fire
or the lark a goddess
or the current angel incisive prodigal
or the dead mime a hyacinth
or policemen the enemy's bad dream.
This is all that will ever count;

that the sun be enough of roundness
that the rock describe the ground
that the priest carry his body high
that the river flow with the swan
that the night bring hawk and star
that some man touch with gentleness his son.

An Incident Early
in the World's History

Nothing is so desperate as a favorite child.
His mother saw a prince in him: Cain,
Prince of Men, blue-eyed, head like a sunflower,
high-stepping, booted, trim as a row of oats,
fierce of arm, Eve's boy.
                        But there was brotherhood
to reckon with and brothers are not simply
double sons, but are apt to be disorganized
and easy to dismay. These two were a trouble
from the start—in the field, one turning
the plow by a rose, the other learning
the disposition of his flock, both watching
the sun. And then there was the twist
of the earth at the fall of rain.
                            The world
had just begun to set its course; the sun rose
daily in a certain place, the hills were
not fluid, nor rocks shivered in the heat:
what was land yesterday was land today,
no more sea lurching to displace the fence
and rust the plow; acres held their bounds
and onions grew deep in the straight furrow.
It was the day of the earth's settling,
of the months of thyme and sheltering trees.

But there was brotherhood to reckon with
and gods to love, and loving gods is often
out of sorts with things and apt to throw the
best of men into a fit. It was a matter
with these boys of the lamb and the vegetable,

which was best, which went up in flame hottest,
what smoke was blacker. It was a choice
of attitude and luck: Abel with his lamb,
Cain and his onion and what was nearer
to the mind of God.
                    And Cain lost.
In the gamble for sacrifice Cain lost and
Abel won; but winning in that family was a curse
and Abel's head got broke apart like that.
All this in the world's newness. Nothing came
before or after it so terrible and Eve and Adam,
used to falling out of grace, leaned from
their tree and pulled the ladder up.
                              Rocks
moved in Cain's acre and in a furrow trim
as a row of oats, Abel's heart lay wound in thyme.

Myth

I knew a man with a terrible obsession
who thought that he was fire
who would tramp the fields in hob-nail boots
turning all the timothy into ash
and all the wild geese into funerary jugs.
He had no fit so terrible as one I saw
at high noon when he turned a page
of Jeremiah and scorched the sands of Gideon
to glass. He was terrible another time
and cypresses curled like shavings at his touch;
roots yielded up their syrups and the sun
rocked in the oven of his eye. He moved
through the world, burning rivers from their beds,
tottering the centers of hoops, galvanizing
snowmen into juggernauts, and pulled up to boiling
the streams of spring. O terrible this booted colossus
this hooting flame who saw all the world
in his obsession and made it do for tinder, flint
and furnace. Hulking in the sun, rattling
among poppies he contended for dominion
in the flaring orbit of his terrible obsession.

Hero

Without the slightest strain
he slew the crude marauder
who standing near a flaming bridge
whelped his braggadocio cry
and was delivered up. Ho!

Unlimited now, he was bruited to
the northerly way. He muddled
nothing, got trapped by no
(however beautiful) lady, in no
(however splendid) garden.
Every, any, thing waked to him;
he was morning, they sleeping flowers.

The tender gorgons, double-headed imps,
rolled hoops, tossed balls into the air,
banked the toothéd wall with tulips,
soared into the trees for a go at tag
with the ape. He came to no patina
in the dirt and held fearlessly
his wand in the face of Dis, hurried
by ten shimmering girls. Lust
did not move in any natural thing.

Simply no fear in him, no meditated
ugliness. Finding avenger dull,
knight barren, seer uncomfortable,
he returned to his place, deep in a grove,
where sang, full breasted, comely birds.

L'Annunciazione

from Bellini

An angel stepping through her window said:
I come to you, a sign from him who sent me.
And leaving then her unbelief she told
the incident from off the sill
and bade it sit before her on the floor.

There was nothing like the fear she felt;
to have a winged and sudden thing
appear to her with not a trumpet or
a trace of wind. She bade him come and say,
if anything would say it well, the news.

He said: I bring you barns and donkeys,
satraps and camel humps, one dozen sheep,
their shepherds and their smell, a star,
a raging king, his sharp knife and a man
who cuts out windows, doors and chairs.

She said: I am used to walking and no grand
folderol of yours will still the flying wind
nor feign trumpets out of silence; connive away,
there's breach enough in any God
to answer you. I have no truck with incidents.

He said: I bring you meadow and winter,
cypress and river, white oxen in the sun,
a boy whose eyes scare dolphins high
as kites; the beautiful mirror of the incessant
zero; I bring you contradiction.

She said: I'll leave you now, you incident,
and from my sight you'll fly, leaving

your wing's shadow caught on that shutter,
your spine breaking the light. I must get
off the dream and back to filling jars.

He said: I bring you flaring squares, circles,
perpendiculars, and trapezoids; I bring you
color from the sun. I bring you
folderol. You'll be Jehovah's honeycomb.
I bring you caravans, a burglary.

She said: I will behave as filling jars were
all my life; I will decide to have a walk,
and incident, I shall not dance again
nor tremble when some doubtful thing steps on my sill.
And fell from heaven then a dominion in her womb.

On Saint Theresa's Difficulty in Keeping Her Feet on the Ground

She would not leap for joy
and told her nuns employ
what means they must
to keep her close to dust.

But God would not obey
and when she went to pray
he picked her up
hood, bib and all and cut

the cloister up with levitation.
She stationed nuns, gravitation
guards she called them,
a wimpled group of ten

to guard her when she knelt.
They waited; at a nod (she felt
her heels kick up) they bound
her with a length of hemp, sound

to a boulder in the wall
and held her tight. But all
for nothing; loose or trussed
they could not keep the just

from rising to the ceiling.
They had a spanish feeling

that perhaps they guarded evil
in that cell. Who pulled? Keel

over once and diabolus perhaps
would roll his eyes; slaps
and knocks of imps; a screech
of angels filled out her peach

with boils; but when she prayed
she felt balloons and strayed
into the light. She roared
and from a line of pillars poured

the guardian ten and pulled
her back to earth. Hauled
down they slid her to a chair
and staked her there

with chains into the floor.
But settled down she was tore
up again and took
on high as fishers hook

a drowsing trout out of his den.
She fought the catch; when
Christus pulled her up she let
her shoulders drop; set

her teeth on edge and fell
at the knees. If it were hell
then hell it was; but she knew
that only God would argue

on the bias; leaving tit for tat
and standing up to all that

leverage, she told the carpenters
to pry her up and loose her center's

howling gravity. No more riot
balked her rising up. In the quiet
of halls of nunnery they saw
their mother floating grandly through the door.

On Turning the Page of a Jeweled Book

For Dorothy Ham Corbin

I turned the page of a jeweled book
and read the singing of a word
held in notes black as spinsters' jade.
On a plain of gold, raised up with bars
of stem, a silver vine spelled "A"
and ran therefrom a runway pressed with
pearl where double "L" speared with
rubies and delphic leaf grew in a maze
of swan. "E" guyed to a griffin
with ropes of ash flared to an almond
tree where angels' bodies filled the page
down to Amen and harassed "L" amid
their wings. "U" was white on white
(like Mondrian but whiter)
and from the lift of the swerves'
crest two fleur-de-lys sprang up
erect as clarinets. In a thicket
three hounds barked a ferret from
his den where "I" complained like a sybil
from the depth. In a rain of runic heads
the final "A" lay cased about with wind.
And when I let the page fall back
(for I went on to search beginnings out)
I heard a sound of horns as when a
quarry tracked to death is stranded in an oak.

The Complaint of a Young Priest

For Charles MacIssac

I hear the golden lion rage,
                      the phoenix
crash in fire where it wished to go.
Krishna on a spinning stick
                a vision
breaks from the greenwood tree,
an egyptian head turns upward,
                    someone
leaves the holocaust and returns to love;
a momentary unicorn passes by the sun,
a flood of robins suffer a partial song
                    and
sheltered by this low fence I lean like
a widow from her porch when a girl in the garden
crushes her youth's body in the night
filling the ground with pain.
                  I cannot
stay within this house; the doorsill
heaves, reason and its geometry
disturb the saints upon the wall
and I recall the deaf child
who wept at the death of birds.
                 When
the sun comes up behind the Lady of the Seven Sorrows
I hear the music of the hoodlum in the night.
I see the flower in his hat.
              The angel
roars in the pleasure of its own fantasy.

Sacrifice is the thing I do.
I am anointed to incur the heat

and not burn; faced with gold, feel the lacquer
and know the hive where there is hurricane
and honey the bee cannot make.

There is other knowledge than the words
the lack of woman makes. What my hands touch
and cannot feel, what my throat tastes and cannot
taste. The absence of the sensual
where the sensuous is all whir and hum.
                                    Twice before
I have complained to the center of the sun; when
I was forced into the sea to find a golden ring
and when my hand had traced itself with slaughter.

Now the third time and the endlessness of it.
Without tune, without alphabet, touched by the certainty
that destroys, I find the white dove
sulking in the tabernacle.

from

Adam Before
His Mirror

1961

The Tree House

All starts in the air where the first
element of the world and place
of illuminations, in the fracture
of its fire, through the roots of the sea,
brings to this household on a cliff

the branches of the sun. Light
crackles in the hive of space, and beauty
holds a crystal to the mind, in this
hippodrome of winds, on this
wooded belvedere.

(But remember the mind at its thermal
joint where the eyes meet the sun
in a coincidence of two heats and cast
a dark cope on the stumbling frog
before your boys pin his brain,

burning as this sun burns.) O cousins
who live in the crag of the sun,
on a precipice of flowers, the center
leaps beneath you where roebuck
and birds in galleries of leaves

bring the world to odds. Bank
the northern slope with roses. Set up
the marble frieze of wild violets and scrolls
upon the light and watch the doric birch pierce
your dreams and the hill ride mightily and flower.

I Am a Falcon, Hooded ...

I am a falcon, hooded, on God's wrist;
my talons hum with the blood of time
and in his greatcoat, belted with a twist
of mail, the falconer in the brine
of harvest stands amid battalions
of the sun, pulling a thread of light.
In leather hood, I hear their stallions,
stomping on the dirt but cannot move, my night
and day so locked and knotted in his will.
I am might, far more than the aerial prow
that breaks through the crust of the wind; my bill
can slam, maul, sunder, force and drill; on my brow
flash the studs and flags of the mind; my ruff
spills light. I am Aeronaut and know the sky;
I am towering animal and sonic beast; I am stuff
of butchery, brim with holocaust; I am the spy
of the ethers, but on God's wrist I am lead;
a feathered spume, brought like a wild,
naked feral boy to race the dead
in the white stadia of the moon. I am mild
pigeon in a cage of hide and though God's vein
beats through my claws, my head in black
obeisance pushes against a leathern pain.
I have murky thoughts and crack
ideas against the paragon. There is no attention
like this attention on the wrist
of beauty, gripping the holy hand, invention
urging the heart to unheard-of skills. I jog. I twist
as fires spring at his head and water grinds
the mortar and ichor of my frame. I hold—
and fly in being still. I see the hind
in the spinning field, the hill kicks under me, cold
flowers yield about my eyes. The falconer spoke
and his belt of mail cracks the air like a thunderbolt.

A Poem in a Time
of Deepest Pondering

There are dreams in my intellect's riding,
stupendous ponderings, that roll through
my mind as mountains roll through
the bucking light.

In the prance of my intellect's riding
a poem breaks through my mind
as a trout breaks through
the cords of midsummer.

The horns and bells of the earth's music
strike through the governance of suns
as cords of water shine in the bucking light
high on the plains of my intellect's riding.

To the Poet Who Concurred in Dragons

Dear Frank, when my mind blazes at its center
and the sun is the rack I lie on and the sea
the whole dream in my sleeping, I think of the
scene at Dornoch's firth I saw one day
riding down from Wick. The hours moved to dusk
and from the horned dark the sea broke through
my discontent and unhinged the runner
in the light who paced his track
like a tiger pacing the small Asia
of his cage. He leaped into my skin
and through the windowpane we crashed
the heather scattering in a raven squall
and on to the end of the firth's black
strand we ran hand in hand turning cart-
wheels in the jet air, splitting
the strata of the faithless sun to find
the center, one cosmos surveying another;
pushing through the water, as come to life
suddenly, a complete monster of the sea,
a dinosaur, brilliant, original, green, head high
in the clouds of my terror, shaking off
the sea animals that rested like a chain
of suns on his back. O I howled in my
own way, rearing up, daring the house of his
brain to open and receive me breakfast-food
or Isaac. And he walked through me clattering
his massive arms, slate eyes, blinking in
the sun and as I brought my hand up to my
mouth to stop a shriek that would have
pierced the center I saw the runner leave

my hand and with a leap so high and quick
I thought I was witness to a hanging he
mounted on the back of that rage of beast
and left me in my track, a wild lad
with a stone in my hand, disappearing
in the black waters, his head flashing
and my runner like a comet riding the waves.

Paolo Learns Gravity at Twelve O'Clock Noon

In the high noon, rocks
it in the air; reels
it through the air;
dredges up the gold
in it; scatters the tribes.
It raises the sun on end;
inches its way through
the foot and knocks
the knees; it apes
the lever; leans out over
the lips of gargoyles;
it nets the lark,
pulls over backward
the head; drowns the
army. It is centrifugal
to virgins; boys trip
on its edge. It hooks
its claws on the hip
and unlocks the turbulence
in rivers; rips up
the rivers and looses
them on the land;
screws down the lids
of kettles; explodes them.
Boom of it scours through
the night; holds up the dream;
dashes it down;
the dream settles and then
breaks through the limbs
to sever the ichor from

the vein. It spins tops;
tops go awry and burn swathes
through wheat; into the brace
of it all things are bent and
in the mortar of light both
intellect and light are crushed.

Two Visions

It was the last vision but one
(as I remember it) at seven
in the morning, standing in the light
of the window I had opened
on the rain. Though it was no vision
then, being early and just from bed,
naked as grass,
a coppered charioteer
with the loam of the sun on his eyes,
it began then, in that light—
thrashing in my ears.

When I walked down the steps
the rain had stopped, the sun
grew on the facade and ivy.
I had an incredible illusion:
Ezechiel, my stallion, bucked on the waters,
the street tipped toward the sun
and the oaken thill drove in
my chest as if a dryad
set her hatchet to the axletree and fell
the wagon, splintered, roots in air
on my heart.

II.

There was Taintor's hill and then beyond it night.
The spell a boy carries in his will, a bright
vine in his crystal blood, sped through him
Like a kite to the brim
of thought where all day dark trees bent

in the windows and bandits pitched a tent,
pennoned, on the hill. I loved him
and found his love uncommon. On the pond the wind
brought him on his way and standing there I watched
his eyes, and migratory birds red, yellow and black
sudden and imperial, broke into a sea of flowers at my back,
and winter, a white barge, boating through the dark
settled in the slivered air its cedar keel. A lark
of bandits had done enchantment on his world,
and like dynamos, from the frozen garden, whirled
a flight of new chimeras chattering in the sun.
I know it was concluded; this was the center. I was undone.

Adam before His Mirror

You are my glove and waistcoat,
my boot and diamond pin,
my starched and pleated blouse;
my anchored collar, my scarf
and woven stocking. You are
the buckle on my hip,
my lacquered heel, my mask
for bees. You are my alb,
my amice and my hood, my walking
stick. You are my lute and drum,
my arbor and my bell, my rain
and sun, my season and my zoo.
You are circle of my hoop,
my scissor and my loom, my junction
and meadow, my sign, my darkness
and my light. You are hyssop
and mint, my crown, my hurdle.
You are the stillness
and the moving in my brain.
You are the span and fathom
of my chest. You are the arch
and vaulting of my skull. You are
root of my hand and exultation
in my reins. You are my image.
I am the stress and raiment of clay.

A Poem to Paula and
a Poem to Ned

I.

I have no thought but one, hot Paula
said. She has the mind of a siege!
The hands of untamed lioness. For her
I left the barricade! Ha! Breathe
on me sweet agate-eyes, fix me on
the sheet like a parenthesis. I have read
books on fire and know the down
and up of the heart and the regions of bed.
Believe me, small face (I left the burning
ship for thee), I've learned marriages and am learning.

II.

The sun reigns. On the hilt of day
seraphs and troops of derring-do
punt through the waters. Wild Ned
climbs the flowering vine. The sun
strips him; he is all flaring;
the stripling of the river,
the fire-eater, all the patience of men
endured, now, so high, such a bird,
admits unto his thought the sphere of summer.
The vine grapples the summit of heaven
and the fruit of the vine is an absolute yellow orb.

A Movement of Peoples

Under the bulb the stun
of rain grinds flowers
out of stone, flame
from marble roots.

Widows, hunters, men
with their sons' singing
in their hearts, climb
past falcons and fall

into the stars. Chaos
tears golden rings away,
silver snakes and opals
from the crusted thigh;

the pyramid, the true stone,
the lonesome king; roam
the Egyptian ladies
in the garden of Tut.

A hand grieves music from
a river. (Likeness of lotus
and aster, green stalk and
a white orient tree.)

The hippo stumbles and a force
of gathering wheels
flips the poles, the world dips
and stands inverted.

A Reflection on the Paraclete

This is Melchizedek's year. I have thoughts
of altars and watch the world like an eagle
drawing his beak on a climber's eye. I caught
the sublimely very beautiful and in my mind,
thrumming, came the paraclete, as in the cave
of Plato came the masquerading light.
The ridge of the delectable mountains
breaks the light and in the cattails and
clover of the Jordan stands the Great Blue Heron.

The Death of a Poor Man

The world is cold by nature. It thinks
of death but not of catafalques and
the heavy wreathed wagon. The soul
of a poor man like Jonah in a sea of whale,
dodging consummation, flashes among
the waters and calls out decretals
of brown bread, hosannas of milk,
and liturgies of beef. The poor man
carried desolation uncommanded by desire
but spellbound by survival he crossed
the lintel into the famous world.

I think of this poor man and his
imperial dream, who dreamed of the sun
flashing unhooded in his eyes, who
imagined heaven as an order of wench
and daisies of chocolate.

The cornflower burning at midsummer
turns the fisherman from the stream.
The river sizzles on the red-hot slate.
In a poor man consummation builds
its holocaust and from the earth comes
a laying on of hands and the instantaneous encounter.

Spring

Nunc Stuporem Meum Deus
Rector Exaggerat. —BOETHIUS

Now God, being my Governor, my astonishment
is increased. I take no long walk but his
compass draws me north, south, east, west
into the four seasons of his wit. The world
is his dominion, expert, bright and meta-
physical. In this assembly of days, my Rector
walks on the plains of intellect,
as the long fires on the sun's face draw
hot meridians on astronomer's glass.

Troubled by thoughts of deities, an Olympian
lady wished that God would come unhooded
to her room, but when God came he came as Fireman
and into cinders went that curious wench.
My Rector comes in the runes and spells of spring
when the dew falls low in the grass
and the morning-glory storms the garden wall.
In the zodiac of April, God, being my Governor,
falls in the mint and flowers of the sun.

The Summer

This is the sun's high exultation
and the ample months of the lark's
preference. Beasts roam without
dreams and there are keels in
the water and dragonflies cross
the air. Children catch
the phosphorescent fly and light
decreases. The Borealis and Zephyr
from the northern sea set off
explosions in the scalding air
and a curious passion, fixed
in the heart by nights of crazy
dreams, cuts the legs from under me
and in the passages of dark,
in the summer's long intensity,
the body learns the canons and conditions
of the heart. (O summer's not
for Manichees.) This is the manner
of the season and from sleep,
current with burning, I wake
to massing butterflies
and my son's hurrahs on the widowswalk.

The Ear in Autumn: An Instruction for the Wild Sara

This is the bellowing place
where the pumpkin sizzles
with sin and a strange wind
moves through the thickets
of the brain. On the top
of the sea waves' spines crack,
and the Sphinx appears
in the cornfield where the ample
witch sweeps across the eye.

Into the skull's bright auditorium,
into the celebrated labyrinth,
like Pierrot from balancing
broken on a parallel of light,
sound, manifest and real,
sets down its noise, hot
with the flames of late September.

It's Halloween, the time of the
apple bucket and the masked child.
Loud in the channels of the brain,
loud in the zodiac,
loud in the night, I hear
the rending of seasons,
and the ice-flow moves like a mast
through the heart.

Winter

In oblique stilettos the winter sun
falls in the plazas and gardens.
The red berry, a scarlet bullet,
hardens on the vine. The beaver
dams the river called the winterbourne
and the hawk glides like a skater
on a storm of freezing air. Noonday flowers:
the wall cracks and roots of chill
trace hexagons on the windowpanes
as if honeycombs were there the summer long.

The matter of intellect is arctic.
                              Hidden
with the clatter of ice and too many freezings
it builds an arena of glazed sound in the ear:
the lean bitter season. Words come slowly
from the throat as if the chords and keys
of the heart forded the space of thought
blind as hunters lost on the polar cap.
Eyes and fingers blink in the sun, the hat
is brought down over the ears and the reign
of intellect collapses on petrified oceans of snow.

Adam's Hymn to His Body

I have high hopes for passion;
for I was once initiate there
and did high jinks in the fashion
of lovers: the hot jig on her bare
belly. My green spine
flowered; a branch broke
through my thigh, time
roistered and sweetly stroked
my brain and fired
the clay in my groin; we grieved;
clay expired
and Omega conceived

the exactions of Adam.
Now after long tournaments
in the arenas of madmen
I've made a pact with glory; torrents
of size and depth rile
on my eyes; falcons in jackets
of mail pace the file
of hunters in my thigh; rackets
of locust and honey bee
bolt on my lips; I've moved
down the face of the sun; the sea
mounts my eyes; I've proved

my body and stand in the light
of spring on the quick earth
where crocus and the night
beasts cut through the dirt
and cataracts of wind drill
like beetles in the shade.

The fields are densities of stone; the kill
of the scythe and the rattler unbraid
this sweet machine
my body; my clock, my element.
O hovering face! O green
mysterium; O high imperial pediment.

Great Grandfather,
Clam Diggers and Homer

I.

His family was like Spaniards
on horses; like prophets
their heads; superb with ladies;
bodies like cherry wood;
necks like chalices and eyes
that caught light as the sea
holds the sun; hunters who dreamed
the malediction of the fox.

But his youngest son, as the ellipse
describes the wave, in the skills
of discontent, drew masts down
the margins of books, calipered hulls
on his bedroom walls, for Poseidon
(rumored in tempests) laid his trident
like wings upon his eyes.

II.

Though his father had no passion
for the sea, he built his son a boat
in the image of the one Odysseus
took to get away from Troy
and one day when a strong west wind
had touched the sound, his boy,
stripped to the sun and the oar's tug,
piloted that barge down the channel
to the sea and in Greek, pure
as the air that touches snow

(the sun of Asia glowed in the noise),
he read of the voyage through
the Dardanelles, past Sunium and Corinth
down the currents to Ithaca where sunrise
and hot temples rose in the burning
noon and the household waited
like traps in the timbered hall.

III.

The clam diggers laughed: "What's this,
pressing through the morning? What noise,
what conspiracy? O Watch."

IV.

At noonday, with bells and gulls
and white sail, a boy, arms red
with the hot light, and an old man
singing glided to the bottom
of the dock where a groom pulled
with ropes grecian music to a standstill.

Penelope, a flower, raised
her parasol and beckoned to the singer
to come up the stairway from the sea
into the blue air where a carriage
waited and a chestnut mare.

The boy who rowed the singer through
the waves, the salt air like a net
of marble on his back, laid his head upon
the oarlocks and dreamed of the light
on waves and Poseidon enthroned.

Two Poems on the Creation of a Statue of a Maenad

I. THE MAENAD TO
ALDO JOHN CASANOVA

I am freewheeling. The unslung hoop
in my blood tingles at nightfall.
Through the briar and onion beds;
through the sacred rivers, up the rocky air,
in the white hazards of the moon,
scooping pebbles for my catapult
I wolf the night.

There is the process of metal in me;
the hardening of the light that gives
the lucent glory to the eye . . .
the dark clatter of gears and the mechanical
clicks of the tissue of fury.
I've watched Dionysus step like a scimitar
through my side.

I know the face of fire on fire.
I've chewed the neck of lambs,
devoured the hare, brought the hot
pyre of my nails to the wolf's eyes,
rooted into the backs of deer with
my toes and shattered quail
with my fist.

I am freewheeling
and follow my blood wherever it goes.
As some men follow fire, others their nose.

II. ALDO JOHN CASANOVA
TO THE MAENAD

In my studio I have built a stand
where I set out a bunch of iron
sticks and clamps to fasten down
the Maenad in my mind. In the focus
of my inner eye, like an apple or
a crystal on a shelf, I reckon
where a Maenad's spine should be
and how the implications in her neck
would suffer under fire.

I drove her into place with double
clamps; arms, legs, hips, thigh,
groin; the raving brow, the vulture
lips; a frame of steel to hold
her skeleton intact for she had shifted
her position once and in my mind
an unsettling took place and the clamps
pulled from the wood and the frame
of steel unfastened in my hands.

It is not easy for a Maenad to keep
still. The rip-tides and bandits
in her blood will not pose upon
a pedestal. But when I clamp down
this first double cord of steel
and set her feet upon a soldered place
she'll rouse the anvil and the furnace
in my arms and I'll predict in steel
and flame the lineaments of bacchanalia.

Through the Steel Haze

Through the steel haze
the bride walks and the sea
is high with stamping
horses.
       The blue of their
eyes bores through the light
and passion is brought to a high
burn.
       O Thalassio.
Bricks crack through the
lion's pelt and the animal
paces the gazelle through
the afternoon.

The sun falls on her hair
and her arms shoot into
the air swinging in a circle
a lasso of marvelous hemp

brought from the extremes
of Asia.
       In the bed of the sea
coral snaps from the sea walls
and one by one the hinges fall
from the locks of the great canals
in the valleys of the world's
center.
       In the boon of glory,
with all her people shouting
in her wake, the bride walks
through the steel haze
drawn by harrowing winds

and the bridegroom's hurrah
to the tumultuous chamber.

Ventus increbrescit.
O Thalassio.

The Tent, the Song, the Sign, the Element

I. THE TENT

In God's tent the sun,
God walks and carpets
and braziers are set out
on his frying lawn where
poles and pulleys,
rings and intersecting
ropes, various nails
and locking joints spend away
in a hot pavilion
where God turns about
and then about again and
stands his ground like a tower
of smoke and bends back
his head and through
the hole in the top of his red-hot tent
two winged bolts of fire rocket from his eyes
and fly red and full of sparks
as if they were bright hackle on a line
toward the depths of the sea,
bait for the blue, the fan-tailed shark.

II. THE SONG

Cut said the owl, cut down the night
Crack said the fawn, crack down the hunter
Lash said the ermine, lash up the owl
Plant said the snake, plant down the hunter
Row said the sailor, row through the night
Blow said the trumpet, blow away the sailor

Pierce said the arrow, pierce through the trumpeter
Leap said the hoop, leap through the archer
Strike said the firebrand, strike down the fawn
Torch said the hunter, torch to the sailor
Sun said the owl, sun on the owl's eyes
Rain said the farmer, rain on the wheatfields
And I rode on the lip of the trumpet in the coop of the sun.

III. THE SIGN

I have brought intense darkness
to light, so stone that it knocked
down fences. I have brought pure thought
from multicolored valleys.
I have touched the sides of mountains
that would have leapt had I commanded
them to leap. The Foscalano would have
leapt and all the animals in Abruzzi
but I commanded only words and the air
bridled like a stallion at the tug
of my hands and to the far and pitchest
fathoms I brought the praise of light
sidesaddle on the sun.

IV. THE ELEMENT

At the nub of radium
at the hollow of the atom
where space is fixed upon
a point of black light,
a jut of green casts into
the beating element
at the nub of radium
seething with dyes and coils
of ether, pointed like stakes,

there at the peak of the atom
where I planted a flag and drew upon my map
the river and the shepherd
one coursing on the ice of the valley
the other leaping a chasm
his crook slashing the air like a scimitar.
I set my blazon in the snow
at this height, at the nub of radium,
where the pennon hums and flashes in a blast of suns.

The Boyhood of Nguyen Van Vinh

My boyhood had an island,
a greyhound, and a white tree,
two birds, a regnant witch,
a pirate and a mystery.

This island had a mountain
with a cave and a craven shrine;
the sun was a mesozoic plant
and the sea was a roaring vine.

This mountain had a nether side,
a dark kingdom and a cliff;
an alert tiger, a sharp rain,
an alphabet and a blue skiff.

I sang high songs of pilgrims
and watched the marvelous light,
as the tiger flexed his ripping paws
and eagles scratched the night.

My island had a den of winds
and a black stag in a walled park.
I dreamed the arts of malcontent
and dwelled in the zones of dark.

But came a day, a fractured time
when in the alleys of the hill
explosions, comets, feats of suns
took brute occasion of my will
and since I feared that I might die
I raised the spritsail in the rain
and turned my blue skiff through the dark
as birds in a white tree shook my brain.

Johanna, the Big Cow

Heu! Johanna is the big cow
looming with milk over
the pen gate and like disciples
on a visionary hike
we move in upon that citadel
of hay and lead her wobbling
toward the stanchions
in the middle of the earth and
bring down boiling into bright steel pails
incredible quarts of milk.
No wonder the barn steams with our breathing
and our thighs bucking Johanna
tingle with the calories of winter.

High to the knees in dung
the eyes braised with cold winds
our spines rock
like rods of iron
in a heaving wall.
Johanna stands intact
as the tug of the electric cups
draws out her white honey
her blanch ichor
into bright steel pails.

Heu! What passion in stanchions,
what procession in cows coming down the road
to be milked.
I cannot remember such high prancing
though once I watched the horses
of a mortal king step into a tent
on a visionary progress
and shake their manes in the sun.

Webbed, Yellow-Billed
and Aquamarine

Webbed, yellow-billed and aquamarine
he was born early to a world of no ducks.
He barked under the willow in the studded air
of bitter flies and nested in the sun.
His companions were dogs; no other duck
he ever knew but himself which conversed
with dogs, learned dogs and followed dogs
throughout the day, though rightly duck
was canine in rhetoric. Nature saw duck
and judged it plumed; this animal knew himself
dog and flew at cats and awaited at the gate
his master's coming. (Though once in the shade
of a flowering window he wished he could tell
the tale of the day he was a swan and encountered
a lady lying on the banks of a wild and singing river.)

from

The Buzzard
and the Peacock

1964

The Toad with the Blind Eye

Often the mind, having no use
for joy spoils in its deliberate
fear and holds all brightness
high, beyond the reach of will
and nerve. To find its balance,
where it can ride free of sound
and sensibility, the mind will
treat the demons to a feast of
spirit and after the long devouring
visitation will lean on its
advantage and be dull and dream,
toss all sweetness and scrape
the barren forms of fear.
These days have been a loss
and a habitation of fear.
I dreamed a friend had died and
for a year I wept in that boundless
grief of sleep: one night I held
a hive of evil languors to my
chest and woke to harbor anguish
all the day. It is a dementia of
my sight, this slow biting silence
of this summer grief. But such
dementia is a cracking of
vision:
to see within that which is
common usage must always defer
to new ritual. It is the highest
flowering of my highest good.

In the pool, at the bottom of
fieldstone steps near a grove

where a green and bronze naiad
rubs the light, a toad, the size
of a strong man's hand flayed out,
sits and twitches one blind eye.
When I dove naked in the pool at
sunrise I felt his crippled foot
and blind eye shut out the speed and
cool labors of my blood and burn about
my ankle a bright green ring of weed.

Vegetable-Life

Where the pulp lifts its germ and the sludge of beauty sighs,
where the leaf pulls the branch to the breathy earth,
where the rind cracks and the buds rust into petals,
where the clove steams and the cinnamon bark spits out cinnamon air,
where roots sweat and the earth boils in curds of steaming mud,
where the stem draws up the seed and holds it like a lamb to the sun,
where flowers rest their animal heads,
there, full throated, limp with seed, lush and smiling is
Vegetable-Life.

To come upon her you must journey through the rains,
and sleep through a night of fish smells;
there must be a dead man in a hot room,
there must be a basket of figs and plums on the pier,
there must be no new ship in the harbor,
there must be the sound of flowers falling upon flowers,
there must be no children swimming in the salt pools.

Where the Flamboyant spills into the vulcan dust,
where the wild pig chews up the door frames,
where the leper kneads his bones,
where the sun is stuffed with guns,
where the water flows like honey from the tap,
where black flies swell in the gecko's translucent belly,
where these are, there is
Vegetable-Life: The Sultana of the Vine,
The Goddess of the Harvest Gone Bad, The Spectrum Swallower.

In an ointment of wild saps, ripe fronds and mosses, tumid wheat,
and barley, Abundance pours down over the head, heavy with pollen
and in the puce interrogation of the harvest
the intellect sprouts leaves.

A Child of Light,
a Child of Dark

One day he knuckled under and they found
him in the garden, a stick in his hand,
dead, watching the world, rigor by rigor,
stop before his eyes. The gardener
covered him with straw, called the women,
who washed him, stuffed his nose with
cotton and bound him to a board with linen
bands. His father took the black mare
and hunted until dark. His brothers
wept in the trees and in the morning
they covered him with flowers and spade
by spade his body jammed tight into
the hillside. The world was maimed.
Its brooding permanence forgot, it bolted
to the tip of everlastingness.

(Each man who finds his way in from the void
is a child of darkness or a child of light;
the harbinger or devourer of light.)

A queerness touched the six years that
he lived. He spoke with darkness and
from the badlands of his dreams told tales
of the fusion and destruction of spheres.
He could not bear the subtle hours and hid
in the dark halls until the night had
filled the spaces he despised. He railed
at mirrors with a stick and filled
clay jugs with water from a forest stream

and bore the sun he caught to all the
animals and flowers in the gardens.

I saw this dead child's face brought to
me by his kin, young Paolo, sixty years
from the year he died. The painting,
hidden in the attic of a country house
for fear of what he seemed to be, was
this child's face, but Paolo, braced by the
free passions of his strident seed, flourished
in the secret ordinance of man and etched
out the harvest of the dead boy's ruined joy.
He is no instrument of demons; dreams
but tells no tales. Though what he sees may be
the ultimate declensions of his sense he bears
it like a stone at the crucial stress of an arch
bears in its thick spatial tact the beauty
of the span, the entrance light, the brigand in the apse.

Counsels to a
Benedictine Novice

I. THE DECEPTION
OF FULLNESS

Be it this or that tense or fine
brick walled garden, the herbs
hoed and linked into bitter tracks.
Be it the brute sun on the copper
tower or the trout flexing in
the stream or the tousled fox,
deafened, sliding through the brush.
Be it the quail beaten from the wheat
building pillars in the air
to hide his ascension from the net.
Be it the rose like a rude stylities
on its stem or the light rustling in
the armor of night. Be it the heart
logged with keening or the mind
stuck on the pike of its responsibility,
summer is a doubtful vengeance
on the snows and will not hold.

II. THE DECEPTION
OF DECREASE

It is brave to flee decrease,
to prick the lean pretense
and burn the barren stalk.

It is a quarry to hawk
hidden, in a blind, backward
to the center, away from the lair

in no abandonment to encounter.

Learn this law: it is to be
shunned. Hold a mirror

to the sterile drone. Be
the yellow-spined nun and hide
like a seed in your linen ark.

III. THE DECEPTION
OF DEATH

The great-gun icicle is tilted
    in the sun. It will find
you out at the expanse where
    hitched to the neck of
the word, self turns, belled
    like a cat on the rim
of God. Enormous levers of snow
    flick mountains through
hollows of black ice. In fairest
    seasons the heart will
tend toward zero. Be defunct.
    Warm yourself, capitulate to the
blaze; await the sun.

IV. SPRING

This is the climate of perfection
    and will not decrease
        except as things
           decrease
           that live

so entirely that the flourishing
    rebounds, one beauty
    and another beauty

fully
without necessity

as things that branch and lower
into loveliness
point on point
of light,
refulgent,

without end. It is Christ that's the season.
As the earth rides
Christ draws in
the reins
taut;

bands together hawks and robins,
daffodils and streams
as the sun rolls in
winged and
praised

by Christ, Primavera's plant bannered
and blazoned. Christ
rides the hills
where snails
prod

light from the buckling dirt
and the plow lurches
stirred to cut.
The furrow
and the sun

shine triumphant in a corinthian harvest.

A Rectification of the Lyric

I know they say it is music;
that it is music we find
in this word we have sought
and carried to the poem.
I know it is song; they
have said it is; time
and the fault of time
is the lyric moat we build
around rime. I have
learned it and to unlearn
it takes my spirit and my
flesh from one field of
darkness to another. Music
once learned is like love
once learned, ultimate
and untranslatable. Now
the other side of music
turns its face toward me,
tipping base and treble clef
onto the rigid void and
facing into my heart the
coin of light that in
seraphic furnaces had forged
a circle, ardent and packed
with the runes and hammered
emblems of the sun. So light
comes upon me in a second
tactic. The first was the crack
to the brain when music
pulling a wagon of light lifted
up its marauding foot
and struck my face with sound.
Learn then it is light

we seek. Not music but music's
interior places. Light. Neither
the aerial light nor the light
that rests upon stone and spring
flowers; not light of the sun
or the autumn garden but light
in the cruse of tile that
moves behind the cliff. Within
the greyhound's pelt. The light
that spoils in the torpid
stone hovering like myrrh
in the quarry's bin.
It is light we seek. Light
at light's midpoint. The mute
light at the dull center
of sound. Light. The bud,
the phrase, the climax.
Exemplum: Yeats, Catullus;
passion and myth cross by
music into light. Or, music
attaches to light like a drum-
stick to the hide of the
kettle. Or, a finger moving
down across water. Like a grove
of birch tempered by sun
into a relief of static fire.

Light has no modality,
no dictum of pleasure.
Light rules now
and rules the poem and music
on its animal of prism
comes blazing down. . . .

"The soul must seek light
by following light; though

it has no place and its
brightness casts a shadow
on this light, less bright
but dazzling nevertheless."

We turn on our heels and
undo the cords and looks that
have held us down and set
aside our children and our books;
burn down our ships;
cast our lines out into the sea
the sea where there is an
unsettling on the waters—
something moves beneath
and shows its eye now and then
above the surface; there
is light above us, beneath
us, at our wrists, over our
feet, light nips at the edge
of the sea; noisesome as
wild geese fish push one against
the other to tunnel into
the trembling reef. There is
nothing left at all, anywhere.
Place has ceased to be; all
herbs are crushed together;
time is broken in the corner
of the eye. Only two things
remain: the circle in space
where the earth had been—
a bright dent on the light—
and over the whole vault
held by the thing it is,
a coil of brightness spells
trumpet alpha and flame omega.

Two Holy Incidents

I. GOD'S FIRST NAME

He washed the dirt from his hands, stripped,
stood beneath the waterfall, climbed
the rocks above and lay upon the hot stones,
stretching into the streams of light
that pulled their tight waters of flowers
and wild birds across the forest. Girded
with a breechclout woven by the hands of
many girls he walked across the river at
the foot of the waterfall and with the ease
of twigs and rose hedges strode through
the wilderness to an altar atop a hill,
its central pedestal tied into the ground
by cords and girders of roots and mica bolts.
From the hill there were steeples, dove cotes,
voices in the barley fields, bells, and
in the distance through the brain flew
two winged, black birds. Upon the altar
he placed avocados, lemons, blackberries,
apples and a coronal cluster of grape; he
surrounded them with wood and at the right
incidence of the sun, when the black birds were
at the crest of their black flight he set
fire to the fruits and vegetables and God's
first name arose. He was called: burning
fruit; burning vegetables; food of black birds.

II. BANTAM COCK

The hens, splashing in their heat,
hie to his lusty promenade. The
widows feel thunder in their claws;
across their blood comes the

cackle of virtue, clicking in the
vermilion plumes that set ablaze
the holy oils. In the unmixed

dazzle of space black birds draw
honey from the brain and out
of the night, from the sleeping barn,
stalks the bantam cock, his belly
and throat sirens in the hens' deaf
wombs. Men and boys, asleep in
towers and caves, wake, and come to

watch his feathered durance coil
through the brood. The leaping
sperm prods the womb; in the warm
hollows of the night a cry of joy
springs from the steeples and
barley fields. And the dawn flashes
wanton on its burning pole.

The Sea—East Hampton

I.

Like a spliced melon
the sea lay knocked open
at his feet. Or he
had knocked it open with
running on its edge,
tumbling the seeds,
doing leaps and
dives on the surfaces—

a scroll of flaming parchment
flinging back onto its
center pin. Or he read it
open, stamping the margin,
distending the vocables
of Poseidon so they
cracked like a cock
swallowing the sun.

Reeled in, the sea
constructs nerves of
light like cat-gut on
the mind and takes
the thrust of driven thoughts
building tumuli of
winds and the winds' hot stuffs
of kelp and ambergris.

A dog-fish, a sting ray
and a blue crab, at
swells and chords of din,
lay fractured on the

searing strand in
boiling rot. The dog-fish
inverse mouth agape; the ray
tooled by flies;

the blue crab sprawled
on the moving sands
sinking into the charged
foundation. He saw
corruption swing on
the tidal lights and
the shifting polar reef
slid beneath his heel

and the lily sea, the grazing
sea, the bitch-wet, bent
on the forged elements and
locked lips on the source
draining the slut wild
to a dry web of air
sucking light like a
whipped shark to the bottom.

II.

He thought he had been born before this birth
in the sea, the child of two water sprites
who mated on a glide of light, near a firth
of coral brush and opaque golden dunes,
their bodies struck in the tow of the lusting
tides where sea-crystal flashed and sea-flares
fell on the eddies and contradictions of the
southerly currents. There, in the angling
of love they drew out his soul from the seed
and generation of the waters, lying on the

charging air like two birds on a glacial mass
pulling a prey of wild fish through lean
and shuttered lights. And when his body burst
its traps and stood graced in knells leviathan,
soul broke through scales and braids of oil
and sailed entranced upon a grazing sea.

III.

Ahead of us a white light made from the
fume and friction of the sea rose at the place
the waves splayed out onto the sand. Mounted
high on the back of the galloping waters the
sea moved toward land where some memory stirred
its blood and sought out the rivers, the streams,
the pools, the waterfalls that gather in their
hides and husks the stasis and tissue
of the sea. This white smoke, this bodied
water, arched its back, and took to the dunes,
girded with the hot ores and sizzling hydrogen
of the tides. When it looked up out over the
line that draws the world into a sphere I felt
the forged images of tidal trumpets and
the keels of embossed and scalloped barges pull-
ing our blood through the battering wild. And
like an eye seeking out the light from a star
that fell in some malediction's flux, the sea
sought out the mountain lake that held a giant
vein of salt like a sliver of seed at the dayspring.

The Heretic and the Dancer

He thought God open; laid out
his brain before him; cut the stout
muscle of his thigh apart; held back
his mouth and pierced through the black
den of his throat to his neck
and skewered him to a table, the wreck
of his ambitions. He stared him down,
his mind aloft in the anatomy of God
where the mystery of the veins, their brown
and copper lights break on his mind like a sod
lifted high into the air where the fork
rings and the pikes pull the sun
into the laggard marrow in the shaft. "I'd talk
in images of farmer and clown, of the dumb

butcher and the simple weavers of bright
colored flags and mats, but the tight
wit and riddle in the mind keep God
locked to the table and the rod
and plier of my trade grind God open
and I fall, thrust by the molten
signs of his bowels, to my saw where devils
gather; where I speak of spirits and
dry theophanies. The revels
of my anatomy go by and God lies, brand
and iron of my mind cooling in the shade,
upon my table, where his eyes blaze
with wonder that his skull once so grave
and lean is broken, amazed

and disassembled: O Lord rejoin again
together wit and passion that strain

the tow of your olympian blood; no place
but woman and flower lament and die; black grace
frets my thoughts and I am become the pyre
of my mind; brow crackles and smoke and fire
reach to my brain's cloven blue
where I rig slaughter and split your marrow bone.
The moon and sun fill my eyes with two
burning discs; beneath my hammer, stone
planes and ruby metal chip and spark. Lord
bind me to your broken center, for my knife
moves in the last strokes of my anatomy toward
your heart where my heart hovers in its little life."

II.

Hurt by one indiscretion, she fell.
And between the edge of life and the edge
of the toothed fires, by an effort
of her back, she leaned on the force that
drew her onto the hot jaws and held there—
while the shades roared
extinction.

Earth electricity forced the light
and the world glowed in the spoil of her stance.
Crocus and wild rose, vines that bear
white flowers and red berries surged up
at her feet as if she'd been touched by aged
and scarred dynamos and currents.
Stars, suns, moons and comets, spheres and
galaxies lurched back upon the void
when the dancer stamped her heel on the sizzling turf.

Hunting Hawks in Ethiopia

On a scarp, two mile high, the arrows
lie side by side in the quiver. Narrow
yellow trees and black pillars lay
on the dawn and on such a plain day
I set out to hunt for hawks. Believe it,
it was my wish to trace a leaf, pit
my dogs at the quarry, walk on to the lake,
but it was a plain day and the great
hawks come down from their cold wills.
Mice fall from their claws; they kill
all rest; hawks are everywhere. In stone bowls
of fire two mock suns hang from poles
of cedar to pull the hawks to earth, run
vulcan in the long waste of the hunt. I drum
the leather quiver and sit awaiting hawks on this plain day.

The air spoils. The sun burns on and I wait
upon the hawks. My dogs sleep and I plait
a net of thorn; my boots kindle. The sun shines
on the high winds and when I tire of repose I line
my sights toward the air above me
to seek the killer I will kill. A bee
on a scalloped band of sound pulls
on my wrist and the hawks, on lulls
of tempest, come down from their cold wills on this plain day.

I walk out into the roaring field. The stone
bowls upturn in the dust and a green bone
of power drives through my peace. Hawks turn
like dice in the tumbling lights as I learn
the law and mercy of the hawk that I will kill on this plain day.

I saw a wild clawing in the air and took
my bow and seized an arrow. A hook

of black pierced the sun and I let
the arrow fly. Hawks everywhere. A net
of black feathers buried deep the light
and at my feet the bird lay dead: bright
the hawk's eyes; bright his plumage
and upon my heart a damaged glory lay and homage
to the wild bird's blood my still blood paid
and I put down my weapons in the night of this plain day.

Corn, Wine and Oil

I. CORN

The late bird of prey counts out his harvest.
The frost the field mouse in its crystal
treachery. A driven heat is upon the burrows.
Corn stalks bring down their silken hammers
on the land. In the pitch fandangle of the
willow the pheasants braid their plumage
in the wind. The fields move out upon the
night lifting high their pollened, lusty poles
like green summer gods. Gold kernels clamp
upon the husk. On the hills and in the valleys
the men bear the noise of the waterwheel turning
the millstone; sacks and barrels fill up with
grain and light, pollened, silken and of the tinct
of gold tips through the bins its immaculate fire.

The loaf swells in the oven. The leaven cracks
and yellow bread stands open in the white stone
kitchen. (I would so knead, pummel and break the
seeds of my ambition that each single angle and
occurrence of my wit—sheaves of wheat, wooden
carts, the implements of husbandry, stallions and
fish—would glow in the bright excursions of the
winnowing staffs.) The radiant cipher of the
loaf, common as brick, keen as a leaf, stands
like the wide sun, steaming, on the sill.

II. WINE

1.

The grape swims in its bright reliquary
as no spinnaker ever swam in the windy
sun and though it has scriptural and nodal
lineage and names it grows best in warm

climates where each year the seasons bring
rain and frost in degrees of unequal
ardor and twist the vineyards to the ground
or strike them barren with the hail that
tips from the sun. At a settling of gold
and mercury red wings stir the light
and the world is blown scarlet and the syrups
and philters in the air cut under the root
and push through heat and mud the grape
onto the hot flank of the branch. The mind,
flushed like a kite brushing the edge of
a comet, moves down upon its roots, salt
on its tail, sharp for the kill.

2.

Thought, said the lions, is the space
the herons see between their image
in the water
and our bite.

Thought, said the hedgehogs, is the space
from the catamount's clubbed
paw to the pistons
of our umber stakes.

Thought, said the phoenix,
is the space between my
eyelash burning
and the flaring sod.

Thought, said the eagles, is the space
between the corded eddies
of the light and
our shimmering fall.

Thought, said the giraffe, is the space
between the steeple of my

body and the belled
shuttles in the air.

Thought, said man, is the space
between my whip and
the bestial skirmish
on the deserts

and upon the hills where the animals
turning on their marauding wills
gather to rejoice. Dizzy, embracing,
howling they turn off into the hollows

of their dark, piped by the nightingales
who sing in the dark veins of the vineyard
and the world's delivered up to the harvest,
the animals and the harvesters.

III. OIL

1.

THE LAST DAY OF ULYSSES
REPORTED BY A SAILOR
He let the oil run over his brow,
down his cheeks and shoulders,
over his hips to his feet where
it was sucked into the howling mountain.
He stood in the dark tent, frail
with victory, the blooded armor on
the dirt, his spear and helmet
lay upon the burlap and golden cloak
he wore in his last attack upon the
savage forms. He broke four vials
of oil into a bowl and breathed in
the sweet green oils like an atmosphere
breathes in the florid rubble of the void.
His body slid upon the air and he

shouted at the pitch vault of the tent
until the wind blew open the tent flap
and he strode out into the raining dark.
His men lay about their dead. Horses
stood in the thunder like tidal waves
and gnawed the wind. From the campground
the half-dead in their doric panic
prepared to storm the slobbering cup-bearer
who lifted up his head above the line of
trees that marked the beginning of the
barricades. The Captain stood upon the
shattered axletree of his wagon, the golden
mountings and jeweled reins hanging in the
bleeding night where the noise of death
hung in the trees, its black plumes and jet
flags blowing on the winds that carried
the waters of the styx upon the spoiled
and upturned olive trees.

                    And in a gesture
that could have been the gesture of a lion
watching the sun spring from the hunter's knife
or an astronomer tracking the final, plundering
star, he turned on the noises and the rains,
upon the horses rocking in the torrents and
walked into the tent where I dressed him in
armor, handed him his spear, oiled in
the ceremony of death and watched with a sailor's
wonder as he cut a hole in the rear of the tent,
turned upon me, touched my forehead with
his chrismed finger and moved out, silent as a comet.

I do not know the end for I fled
through the camp, and hid deep in
the hold of my ship where I stayed
till sunrise. When I woke the day

was bright and in the sky I saw
a glittering heel budge the firmament.

2.

The wife drops the radish
into the wooden bowl
and the green oils cling to the skin.

The poet spears the word
in the clear streams
and the stones glow like ripe olives.

The child stands his hoop and from
the tree races through it
and the green leaves spin on the olive trees.

The poet stands his self and from
the light leaps over it
and the olives sing in the grinding vats.

The schoolboy walks on the white fence—
and pickets and palings hold him kindly.
And from the olive grove the olive branches
float in their green oils.

Intellectual man casts a line to the
sun-cliff and pulls it tight.
The green-sap tightens in the pit
and the olives suck in the tawny spices of the sun.

Watch the green oils and the olives and the olive groves
when the sun mounts the branches and greenolives,
blackolives, floating in the black alleys
of their leaves, fall into the press that
trundles through the groves pulled by two white
oxen bearing the red signs of fire on their horns.

The Virgin's House

This is a well guarded place.
A boy with a bear on a chain
sounds a tambourine in a grove
and lying in the road,
his knees up, a shepherd pipes
on a wooden whistle; below,
the drag of the sea and a line
of camels strung with bells.
These are the watchers who report
all visitors, especially hunters.

Here the air begins to flower
and a cage of hogs, wire-snouted
and toxic in their slime,
have the odor of the heart.
(There is a sanctity that has
no oil and balm but dirt.)
It was here the Virgin came
to wait the dreamer of her womb,
in a grove of bears, on a road of whistles,
where light was stem of the sun.

This is the place called Mary's House,
in Ephesus, where hills mirror the sea
and rocks mirror the earth
and the earth mirrors the precious
minerals of the sun. There was a lady
companioned by a youth with
abandoned eyes and bright memory
who came with chattels and a cat
to rest here: from lights,
from the worshippers.

Place is of the mind; in the stormy
latitudes that cross between the

brain and the graven winds there
are crevices and heights that prepare
for tombs and cataracts the body,
as it moves off like a lamp
into the shafts of space. House
and house's beams and vaults
must repair unto the mind as
images of mountains drive into climbers' rope.

On a day of flint when the hogs
put dents in their wire cage
and the air caught in the cracks like grass,
tambourine and pipe sounded
in the grove and stilled the winds;
bears set up a stamping and a yell
for the Virgin drew her hands
across her eyes when a visitor,
white as broom, in a hunting coat
lifted the door latch and drew back the bolt.

The Dark Dialogue

"I had a dream, I tell you, I had a dream
naked at the rim of hell.
I descried a whirlwind."

I said: "Well enough." Pinned
him with my eyes and asked
how hot it was.

"It singed my palate
I closed my eyes and it
singed my skull-bone.
Out of my mouth I cried."

I said: "Incredible and was it
pestiferous?" (A High Groan)
I set him down before me.
By his hair I brought him
down.

"It glazed my eyelids.
Maggots at my temples;
a heavy dew fell
on my skin. Outrage, I cried."

I said: "No blessing."
"My thighs and belly
burned through; a sulphur
tide gathered at my feet.
'Break, Sham Hot,' I growled
at the diamond wind."

I said: "The assassin pursues.

Sit quiet; lift your feet;
you make the floor smoke."

"All the colors of pain
burned in me; the white
and the black and the red. Aheee
how the jaw-bone cracked
and the neck bent."

I said: "You are deformed."

"When I thought my front-brain
would fall into my mouth,
I heard the sash go up.
The sun ranged on the wall
and I saw you standing on a lake of frost."

I said: "I am Zero."
And closed him four-square round
with ice.

As It Was Then
It Will Not Be Now

As it was then it will not be now;
nothing in excess; equilateral;
row upon row of similarities;
equidistant; nothing angular

or bestial. No sound but its
corresponding sound. Every
thing harmonious. Matchless.
The walls unbuttressed; spiders

wove webs paragon; each thing
its place, sunlit, and hard.
But when we lay down naked
and straight, my arms

crossed upon my chest, your
hands resting on my belly,
our heads tilted toward
each other, then all was patterned

and consentient. But things would
be as they are now and I called
upon your soul and you delivered it
sumptuous and unlimited.

It was then as it never was:
everything in excess and when
the nightbirds perched on the
egg of the sun we leaned upon

our souls and the elements,
first hydrogen and then ice

helium named themselves and all
things were as they never were.

It would be as it never was before
and logos, multifoliate and
winged, chained my genitals
like anchors to the burgeoning suns.

The Burning Bush

This was a caustic bush,
tilled in adamantine earth, shielded
    from women and the moon,
locked from the florid current of spring,
    branching in darkness, its leaves
falling like chains in the shadows.
    It was harrowed by the viper,
who pets his venom under the granite arch.
    Camel's dung first fired it.
Bedouin girls, their masks hung with gold,
    chimed by it; the gazelle lay
upon it in the night; the ibex wet it
    with his tongue. It was
scanned by the lizard and
    razed by the sun that clipped
its buds with its scales. It bloomed
    in the wind when blood
cracks through the arctic and sends
    scarlet gulfs through the light.
It would not burn until mind
    conceived its dark genus; it was
no plant to cope with seasons; the brain
    its muds and rains and winds
was the burning of the bush. No blackberry,
    no herb or specie of rose
could reach its roots to the brain
    and thrill the hot vein that
floats on the oils and waxes of the soul.
    When Moses came shod with discs
of salt upon a mist
    growing through the sand he stirred
like a spring and from the center
    of the mist a root moved

toward his mouth and from his mind
    a lean branch of flame, pointed
and in the shape of a plow, cut
    the mist and bloomed the burning bush,
in the brain of the prophet
    in the Arabian shale. The plant spoke
in a forked tongue, green as a Vegetable God.

The Architect Speaks
to the World

I will break my mind with joists,
winches and hammers: damn
poets, painters and music makers.
I'll have BUILDINGS!
                    The world
breaks at my drill: saw, nail
and geometric noise fall
low lying fences, thickets and
flowers.
              Ramparts, vaults,
buttresses, piers and ziggurats
center the sun like a capstone
on the land. I say BUILDINGS
to prairies, cliffs, fields of cattle.

The hewn stone plummets, swings
in an arch that grinds the
arena of combat on the grain;
into the slag of bolt and crystal
I drop the sundering wedge
and scaffolds and cupolas
gape like glowworms in the ditch.

Throw your eye on that dome:
see the light scud across the
ellipse, crack on the warrior's
bow and fall on space I've
squared and split. Believe it:
space is a BUILDING and I will build it.

Written on the Occasion in Cairo When a Man Rode through Heavy Traffic on a Bicycle Carrying on His Shoulder a Pane of Plate Glass Five Feet Square

The thing in itself is often not the image
of the thing nor its metaphor. The thing
in itself is perhaps never more than the wrong
way from one particular to the universal of
another sort; from the country where there
are known circumstances to one where there
is the disproportion of all reality. The
fracture of the thing upon its metaphor is
a new violence, a new intermediary of intellect;
the thing falls out of line and is surprised
in its unconditioned solitude by the metaphor
with its last and perfecting vanity. It is
an election of fires that moves the heart
to its massive, transient laughter.

The Black Lady

Her face leans on my face
and stops the body.
A black cannon bombs the law
and shoots down the fences of the sun.

Her body leans on my body
and stops the blood.
A black sea twists its loins
and pulls upon the surface of the brain.

Her mind leans on my mind
and stops the eyes.
A black moth knocks the light
and lifts the net from the sparking hive.

Her bead leans on my head
and cracks the jaw.
A black skull breathes out fire
and burns the drifting waters and the light.

Her loves lean upon my loves
and sails explode.
A black wing cuts the heart
and eagles rush like knives upon my face.

The Teacher

To Jeremiah Durick

There is a line—I have seen it
between chicory and thistle—
connecting one thing of beauty
with another.
                    The leaping arrow
blunts the light, so our minds
press on music in that trajectory
to a point in the air where
the needle of thought pricks
the wall of reason and we stand
like bridegrooms on the verge
of beauty.
                    I climbed toward
light through you, a lecherous
target for all music and final
rigors. I loved your hands
and your philosophy; those were
the days when I'd have laid
my life down for your voice and
when I looked up from my book I saw
that I could see through bread and
honey, the long blindness of my
just calamities being suddenly
unloosed and I was free to linger
on the truth, couchant on every
swell of light.
                    Now my greatest
Teacher, dead and closeted away,
your brawn and glory locked in
chains of ash and root, I dream

your hands and your philosophy
in the hours I draw a line
(in the mute talents of my blood)
between one thing of beauty
and another, as the leaping
arrow blunts the light.

A Beauty Meditates on Beauty

Who knows this ceremony? Beauty guards
my body, paints my blood, is my bone's
joiner; my breath's keep. The earth,
fired and uprooted, brings its syrups
and hot colors to my skin. Chains of
jade, milk, gold and silver, the small
gut of the worm, feathers and pelts
from a wild country hold me, baroque
and spoiling in her barbarous net.
Though I hold my mirror far from the
wind and metal lights, I know that beauty
is the way I'll die—though all men
die with beauty in their arms.

As the chase sends the hunter to seek
the buck torn with lightning on the
cliff and the hound to the mad red fox
chewing up his madness in the pyre
of the oak, so I lie down with beauty
and rise up to feel the deviate lunge
of my spine.
        In the fancy days, I knew
that beauty had no law that doomed
weird girls to dream of toads. Pocked
hearts and those that beauty stuns come
like summer clove and the sweet wild thyme
to bloom and then they crack and are
undone. When I die I pray I'll rot
among the ugly and their kind and when
beauty hacks my soul out of her loathsome
net, in that frigid journey to the pitch
I'll jab the ass of that pale bitch who
laughed me with her dazzle to my grave.

In Honor of
the Mother of God

I do not know how I should call her

Pelt
White Door

In a world of toads and electrons
how does man call this drudge of the
ghostly bird

Kite
Wagon
Fish Net

She did not seek
the wedding horn
She formed integral
man who cannonaded on the
wide planked roman light
like wassail
with a sensuous rabbinic gait

He was immaculate as the sea;
his voice cracked with the nap
and rattle of the maelstrom

Loom
Bark
Syrup Bucket

She was the spirit sail

who leaned into the wind
spinning like a green vine

White arrow
Spice of Eden
The Sovereign Wizard of Seed.

Stonegrave, Yorkshire

Spring, 1963

The Man of the Tribe advances over the
brick walled fields in a casque of hides,
bolted in a pelt ribbed with weeds dried
in the brackish sun. About his waist hangs
a stone hammer; the skins of his shield
are scratched with the names of the first gods.
The taste of intelligence is on his lips
warm as the blood of a goat when its belly
flies open to salty teeth and the smell
of the veins chokes the eyes. He moves
from hillock to hillock, vanishing down
into a valley, up, over the crest of a field,
onto a plain, through the wood, snapping
the low branches, tearing up the spring grass,
to the palisades of the Village of Wass
where alarms of burning oil flashed
in his hooded eyes. The law of things
like a drugged light creaked through his
painted brow as ladies of the Hadramaut
beckon to traders in wools and holy parchment
to bring the tack and spoil of play
to halls of grit. He heard the ring
of his voice on the rain, saw the maps of conquest
and took to his mouth the speaking grains:
in the mind's accord all was plenum as he stood
in the axial shadow, in the high summer of signs.

The land rested. The sky atop the brown hills
was buoyant and floated on the light.

To walk toward those hills and to come upon
the clouds at the crest is to remember how

it was to walk on a fence or along a pier out
into the sea; to balance on a log and ride
the waves on a summer current of winds; it is
to swing out from a tree and stretch on the prow
of a dinghy and drag a hand through the waters.
Atop these hills there is no precipice
though it seems chasms fall beyond the walls
where the next field, another hill and sky float,
where the legs stride out upon the earth. Along
the fences sheep graze and in the bronze day, in
the Valley of Wass, the mind knocks against
the heart with green budded staves.

To the Memory of Lydia Hoffman

When she danced upon the counter of his bar in Flatbush
her husband beat her and she came to us bearing
a scar upon her cheek: she limped and wore a flaring
red hat with white flowers on the crown. I was
four months old and she drove me through
the nursery like a whip, oiled my crooked feet with
olive butter and shined my father's hunting boots—
she was in our house like a furnace; she roots

now in my memory with the pikes of her agonies.
She devoured us: we ravaged her, left hoses running
in the gardens and in the afternoon lay drumming
on the attic floor above her room where she rested
after a morning of our barbarities. Lydia wept,
bent over tubs, baited traps and prepared the meals:
we mauled her with cats, muddied shoes and toads:
she studied us as a priest the victims in the sacred grove.

Lydia was born in Zurich in a farmhouse on the river Sihl.
When she was seven the farm caught fire
and burned all day in the white pool of winter. As the pyre
reached to a skin of flame, at the moment the center
timber fell, her father rose up burning on the roof,
black and dumb and threw himself into the air
and fell spinning on the frozen ground:
his neck snapped and he thumped the ice. The sound

of a great wickedness pulled forever at her head
and she dreamed of high flames on mountain tops,
of falling gables and a figure burning in the ruts
of a frozen field. She was queer and hurled dishes
at my father, drank gin with straws and sang the songs

of Heine in the kitchen. Lured by her fury to containment
we learned the dark directives of her mind:
she was broody, lashed and crippled and heard the whine

of thugs in the maple grove, saw poisoned water
in the tap, smelt fire on the stairs. She raged
and cursed, limping through the halls, caged
in her agonies, her brow horned with scales of pain
that spat in the marrow of her legs. But in the spring
when new wheat and cold streams heckle in the field
and animals break down the fences of their pens,
when the field mice and vipers, cocks and hens

yield to the sun, Lydia led us to a hill
where we watched the world break its green egg
as she swung us, hopping in circles, on her game leg.
But as we grew older she grew mad and wandered
in the ice and weeds of winter nights carrying
a lamp to seek a child she dreamed our father
burned and cast into the pool beside the barn
where it lay swelled with toads. Our white farm

house was our priming shed and we were transformed
there into those who knew the ways extremity takes hold.

In her last days, upon a tilted bed, bold
as a withered kore she was baptized and died with
a medal on her nightshirt in the odor of the holy oils.
She lay in her coffin clean as dough, hair in
ringlets, her nails painted red, a peacock power
croaking on the coming lights: from the cool tower

of her rest she calls her father from the chars
of glory. But through the burned shadows and floating

timbers of the mind, Lydia walks, a peg-leg fury, bearing
the sorrow of a great compassion. She stomps her
foot above me, pulls up her sleeves, digs in her
heels and swings the hook and grappling line
to strike the final, mating blow
of first calamities: of the father, the flaming rooftop, the gaping snows.

from

The Harvesters' Vase

1968

To Bernard the Huntress

For Sister Bernard of Tarrytown

It's the long field that gets you:
the hedges and the fallow edge of the wood;
the moss on the fence at the junction
of the crossbars and the upright posts.
Then the cool wood the hounds hit,
their snouts boiling with foam
to bleed the fox from his hole.

You know how it is, Bernard, when the morning
is not much of a thing but the faint blaze
of willow on the bark of the lawn. From the oak
doors of the Manor you step, dressed in
a black skirt, your hair bunched
at your neck, boots done to a peat shine
that flouts the mare's skin, dull enough to go
like brown gold with the sapphire whip hiding
in the depth of your scarf. And the surge
before the jump when the beast sees the stop
in the field, hauls up its knees, lets fly
its back and you are grafted there, an extolled wing,
that springs exulting from his mane.

Paolo Climbing Down through a Tree

For Paolo Lorimer

He is off to wring the neck of the luncheon
chicken and cut the throat of Sunday's
rabbit. A knife between his teeth
he steps down from the balcony
onto the top branch glowing like
vengeance in the leaves. The roadway
steams. His shadow falls from the branches
breaking up the skin of morning.
I reflect him in my heart, this child
carrying weapons of supper. I carry weapons
too between my teeth, the weapons of will
and music.

       We increase in animality.
The harvest grows in the sun between
the double gates of death and greenery.

The Memorable Thing about Love

The memorable thing about love is
that it consists of talk rather
more than silence. One of the marks
of lovers is that they must talk
to one another. Christ is, by that
token, the greatest of lovers.

Love too is known by its silence.
It is a mark of a lover's stance
that he is struck dumb before
his beloved. Christ then must be
the finest lover and beloved.

Love is understood by the ways
it discovers to refer all
things to itself, by the sorrow
of its duration, by the
lament in its dearest moments—
in elation, in departure.
So then it must be that Christ
is the most accustomed of lovers.

The Blue Shutter

J'ai prononcé le mot réalité. Il faut encore bien s'entendre sur signification de ce mot: c'est pas un fiction, c'est une réalité. —PÈRE DE REGNON

It opens, closes, opens and freezes
on the blue shutter surging, hinge
and pine, against the stone walls and
spider lights of autumn. The eye dreams
in its sanctum of bone. The shutter
rumbles against the skull, swings inward
and halts against the bramble of the eye
like a hand holding in the dusk a shield
of hides. At the burning edge of the iris,
circling the heart, the shutter opens
like a leaf fallen on the edge of bright water.

The Prayer of a Friend
Whose Loves Are Sorrows

I do not ask for bread or wine.
I have the sun and air.
I ask for a knife to cut my will,
for an axe to cleave my lust in two.
For implements razor bright
and lithe with edge: those
nourishments I lack
and beg them Lord of you.

I do not ask for virtue
or the well-steeled soul.
I break from still and dumb.
Uproot my loins. I ask your
wrath, your storms, your drum
O Lord upon my skull.

Upend my bed; set angels
at the doorposts of my room;
bind my hands with thorn,
my sex with thunder.
When my love, like bait,
passes by me in the street
sucking fury between his
thighs and I am bolted there
by love to taste his flesh,
then, Lord, lay me upon
the limits of your wrath
and when Mad Hierarch
would etch me like a scar
into the ice of his
erotic jaw, descend and lift
my body from his mouth.

Toward You I Fall

Toward you I fall though I do not wish to fall.
Toward you I bend my head though I do not wish
to see the light upon your brow. Toward you my
hands reach out. My neck and back seek you in
the dark. I see your body on the wind. It leans
upon my hand and upon the windowpane like frost.
At your waist I watch the moon rise and the lowlands
slide beneath your belly. Waterways mount your breasts.
I snap like green wood. I loose the field.
You bear me off. I lie upon your body where I fall
like a face and plumage on a blooded shield.

Looking Upward at a Waterford Glass Chandelier

For Nora Mathews

When I look upward into that tuned sky
of the glass blower's gut, each baked
drop of running heat brings to me
the time I was a boy and woke to find
the world aslant with wickedness.
I walked into the forest and sat on the bank
of a pool where the springs that lay across
the bottom sent up cold rings of peace.
Trees stood on their tops; in the moss that
clasped the banks, ladybugs and red berries
moved like small horns and pricked the
soundless walls of trees. When the sun
had soared to her flaxen perch and fell
into the pool's cast net, a ripe crack
of yellow feathers tapped the power from
my eyes. Turn now, quickly, to the west
window where the sun has moved over the
brick walls of the vegetable garden and hangs
there to salute this sister sun that pours
out above us in a volley of glass wings.
O dear Nora, hear them, how they greet each other
in this coupling of lights.

The Harvesters' Vase

For Sloane Elliott

All things are gods.
                    After having accomplished
the embarkation of the lion there was the
unearthing of the orange sarcophagus and the
polished stone gaming board and its tourmaline
counters. And it could not be but a sign of their
desire that they painted fish upon their corpses'
hands and necks.

                    The entire world for them
was gods.
                    At a harvest festival, fifty men stepped
into a line of march and crossed this black steatite
field on the ripe earth; the wheat shoots were
sharp as crystal on the naked feet of those gleaners
of the Wheat-God's pleasure.
                                        The wine pouch flew
from man to man. The sheaves' dried seed fell
and stuck to their brows; their skin pulled tight
across their skulls, for the harvest was hard and
winds curled that summer from the air harrowing
their bodies into craters where they stood all day
collecting the ripe lava of the fields.

                                        When
the temple came in view, cocked on the hill
preened and unconsolable, riot struck the
harvesters in their inner ear. They fell into a
run, belching, clutching at rocks, bleeding,
their bodies bare and black in the sun's mill, and
slammed into the sacred magazines where they upturned

jugs of wine and sacred creams and muted by this
sacral fancy in the steatite thunder of their feast,
they climbed into the precincts of the
Mother Goddess of the Countryside who ran
out of their ears and mouths like a heavy wine.

Plenitude

Where gulls ride
the floating plains
of the sun,
there
is plenitude.
Plenitude
is in the flowers
of the sea,
in the haze at the shell's
edge.
Plenitude salts
divinity
when roots' abundant rods
are heavy
on the earth;
when the lion's mane pulls
down the high grasses.
When the seed rocks
in its cylinder
of privileged
dust
man is proven plenteous
in his courtship.
Beasts are plenitude
of the branch
they slumber on
as the light is in the leaf
it traps.
When the moon
is up,
tides, deprived of harbors
twist their briny necks
to the skies.

A Conversation between Willa Muir, Rudolph Nureyev, and Ned O'Gorman about Excess

Nureyev.   How many leaps within the leap?

Willa.   Let the end of the thing done
be the leap to the crossed beams of white light.

Nureyev.   I shall leap twice into the crossed beams
of white light. Within the rudimentary leap
I shall etch two uncaused fluted turns.

Willa.   No. Do not hitch eight horses
to a four-horse carriage.
Two uncaused fluted turns
is eight horses.

Nureyev.   Had I no legs, no arms, no
triggered thigh and arch
I'd leap through hoops,
not through crossed
white beams of light
that span the middle of the scene.

Ned.   We are grafted to excess.
Beat alphabet get a vine.
Beat vine get a lion.

Willa.   Vines and lions are eight horses.

Nureyev.   I'll climb vines and ride lions
as the bull-dancers rode their
fancy bulls through Cretan stockyards.

Willa.   Excess drains blood of salt and bread.
         Edwin cooked excess.
                          It did not cook him.
         It cooks you both.

Nureyev. (Ascending)
                          I cook space.
          I eat the savory meal of over and above.
          I make simplicity from what is ripe,
          and take from abundance and return it chaste and
              recollected.

Willa.   The shaft bends. The wheels cannot pull out
         of the mud. The beasts confused by
         force beyond the reins' strength twist back
         the hub and spokes and pull the rings
         straight at their foaming mouths.

Ned.   I hear a rhyme
          descending.

Nureyev. (Descends)

Willa.   The superstructure keels.
         Form has run amuck
         with the orbs.

Ned.   Abundance scooped from abundance
         yields abundance.
         At the incidence where fancy and
         excess appease the accidents of form
         we
         begin.

Nureyev. (He lands.)

The House of Victoria

For Victoria Ocampo

I deed to you this Mycenean blue axe
that lies dreaming on the floor
near the window. A red-bloomed tree
fell athwart the light when
the last shutter slammed back from the walls
and I stood in the will of the
rising morning sun. A trophy for you
to set among the chattels. It is a fine
piece. The handle, one and one half
feet long, is dark ebony, carved at
the top with four gold rings set with
colored glass–gray, ruby and gold. The
stock is simple; at the base
is a small inverted v and at the center
a lemon sun looks down toward the blade.

The sun is a little higher now. I feel
it on my chest. The axis of the May
sky tips me forward on my feet. The axe
is in shadow. My legs astride it and the blue
metal shifts to darker blue. But the blade
is the treasure I give you. You'd
understand that blade. It has a double
cutting edge, in prim, bloody arcs
at either end of a flat blue field.
(There is a rise at the center
where the neck of the warrior feels the
last thud of life.) I bend now
to lift it. It lies across my hands
with the rigid weight of a lion's mane.
The black pelt of the handle burns
my wrists in the gaze of the lemon metal sun.

Take it and let it sleep among
your friends who grow like emblems
of a dynasty in the rooms of this
great house. Perhaps Stravinsky or Valéry,
Tagore or Mistral, who walked with you through
the aisles of your tropical park, would
think it precise enough to exclaim one
blessing on it. (It will bite the wood
of the cherry table in the tiny drawing room
and settle on the household in one gleaming cleave.)

The room is a blade of vegetable and flower.
The bowl of jasmine mounts the wall
into the white wooden ceiling. A jug of
rosemary catches the jasmine in the spicy yell
of its gentle, fragrant stems and the curtains
made of fine linen with florid scrolls at the edge
blow inward and catch on my bare shoulders.
The axe has gathered the sun
in a nub of blue heat at the center of the field
of slaughter. It pierces to the heavy armor
of my soul. I hear it lift into the air,
hover there and then descend, with the burning glint
of a wing, to free my tongue for this song.

Signs

The world is signaled.
Look. White flags on doorposts,
red flags on barns
and in the tavern a tin cup
chained like a bible
to the table.
O tin cup, bits of cloth,
boots that charge
between the doorposts
to hoot of
wars and harvests . . .

These stop the traveler.
He sees the white flag.
A dead child?
A marriage sheet?
Pestilence within?

The white flag hangs to say,
"The bread is done."
"New bread within."
The housewife broods above
the table. The new loaf
stands before her, a crusty,
steamy temple making brown
advances on the walls and floor.
Heat rises from the
open oven door.
(White flour on the
underside of new bread
is dry and pure.)
Mice slide across the empty
flour bin.

———

The red flag hangs to say,
"The calf is dead." His belly
open and his bulk strung up
in the slaughterhouse.
Blood from the neck
slides like dew
off the shiny hoof.
O severed head of calf
skinned to crystal
nerve. How your muzzle
hairy and wet shines
on the butcher's marble counter.
O the leg, the neck,
the glad, dumb mouth, the small
curved beginning of
a horn . . .

Go watch it dwindle
into meat and buy it for
your table.
The flags are signs
of commerce
and bid gold and silver come
to hallow them.

The chained cup says,
"Drink but do not steal the thing."
The crock beside the cup is
full. The wooden funnel
hanging by the cask
is wet with gin.

O smell of garlic
in the palm.

O sea urchin
and the live crab within
the husk.

O stink of iodine.
O black seaweed and salty syrup
of the sands on
the umber spikes.

O bowl of jasmine.
O jugs of rosemary.

A herdsman, spurs about his boots
like silver thorns,
a soldier with his breath
cut short
charge between the doorposts,
gouge out their mark
upon the table
and shout,
"All life is blest."
"There is new grain in the bin."
"Juniper berries ferment in the barrels."
"Ovens swell with fire."
"The calf slides his neck along the axe."

And
alamos, erect as sprays of
wind, breathed upon the night
as the dry funnel hissed
for gin and the chained cup rose
like frost
to the herdsman's salty lips.

The Galilean Light

For Molly Finn

St. Peter's Fish, the flat hot bread,
the wheat within the tow of the sun,
the light upon the fin, the crust,
the stem of food, O Molly, lizards
move like clocks across the stones:
silence falls upon the surface
of the sea, dissolves like bread
upon the white fish's eyes in Galilee
where Jesus brushed the pollen from his beard.
A bird flew up from a rocky field,
brown wings, marks of leaves upon his feathers;
it seemed if Christ had scared it up returning home
from drinking minted tea. Goat, flower, fox,
lamb, river bed, field, moon and borderland,
in the rough tissue of Galilean light
where the bees from Tabor gather in their glee
when hives are filled with honey,
the sleep of flowers on their wings,
fall in shadows blue and green as rain upon this land
and sea where Jesus took the air in Galilee.

The Paralytic

I have waited now ten years
to hear this pool speak through my tears.
Legs bent under me,
my neck a hangman's noose. I cannot see
but what the inside of my eyes' watch
of the brain's flood. I am a golden face
beneath an iron mask. There is a case
to be made for me: ten years on this
pallet; each time the angel hissed
through the surface some rich man
knocked me over and stepped, rotten in the can,
puce lipped, into the green water
and stepped out pure as any rabbi's virgin daughter.
I stay a wreck on the water's edge;
nose running, face agape and no pledge
from the priest to move me up one place
closer to the edge. That bastard takes money for the race
into the pool—a change of pallet to the right
or left—and when the angel coughs upon the light
he who was quickest with the gold falls
splashing to his cure. I'll jump the gun some day,
swallow the burly pollen of the pool and rise up
like a fern from moss, lithe, reposed, floating, erect and cool.

Hands

Never was such a portent as this love,
even as prophets dream, so impossible
to reckon. There was space and then
no space was but the vine of our hands
clasped together tight as the press about
the blazing grape. Raw salts, muds of herbs
and fossil, germs of ore, steamed from the
black yeast of the earth. When your
fingers pressed upon my eyes, muscle and
vein wheeled between us in a small typhoon.
We brought our wrists to the other's lips
and fell asleep like two sounds on the risen
bank of a coral reef, as saffron fish nets
swung on their poles toward the sea.

To X Who Never Existed Except in Reality

The wilderness I brought her I brought
in arms that sang like sheaves of wind
to lie across her face. I leaned into the
steamy target of her soul, took my place
above her and descended down like the
mariner who follows the phosphorescent tides
all night and comes at dawn upon the perfumed
sun resting on a dolphin's foamy back.
And when we reached the randy climate
of repose I lay upon her in the delivered
glory of our flesh as if I never knew but
hours at her lips and days above her
turning like a windmill to lift up the first
spume of water toward the infertile sun.

Haircutting

"Come, untrimmed path, and sit upon that stool."
She unfolds a sheet and covers him from head
to toe. Between the left ear and the skull
she lops. No hound chasing frogs into a hornet's
nest came out less chewed than he, Luis,
who looks into a triptych mirror and concedes
that art had lost the day to fancy and his wife's
economies. A thousand spiders scud across
the floor. A scar atop the ear, a neck too bald
for tact, the forelock gone, the crown indented
like a saw. "Once," he said, "a Corsair and his
mount assumed the enemy asleep but met him
armed with candor and a knife upon
the lunar battlements of an incompleted strategy."

At the Tomb of Ha'ari

In the Galilean zone of the heavy Eastern sun,
the lion whelps gather at the blue grave to pick
his brain.

The light holds down the four corners of the earth.

The lion whelps rend their cloaks and fall muttering
in the dust.

"Izhak Luria, Rabbi, The Lion, who called up the seven
shepherds of Israel to read the Torah on the Sabbath,
leap now from the eclipse of light you kept in a band
around your hat, creep from this blue box and tell us
the forms-of-what-is-not."

"Schicinna," he had said, "is the eking out of Jehovah's
beard through the world." He said it, standing on his
right to say it, upon the pavement of the thresher's floor
when the wheat had been spilt through the stone mill
like blood.

From nowhere came sound: the cracking of muds, the jingle
of bells, the bellying forth of a pomegranate, the fall
of stones through water. A field of wheat sprang from the
rocks beneath him.

The valley crept on all fours into the synagogue. Ha'ari
unrolled the light around his hat and found on the edge of
the scroll, the waters of life and a fish swimming in them—
dorsal fin white as sandstone and petal of a daisy. It
slid against the text that was linked in the Rabbi's
dream-of-what-was-not-but-was-to-come, to the flesh of the sun.

———

A hag with yellow braided hair who kept the keys squinted
at the lion in the shadow of the screen in the women's
gallery. When he lifted up his eyes to call the presences
not there but possible, the walls of the room screamed, the
air leapt for joy. Grapes fell from the thick arbor
on the roof. The seven-branched candelabra broke like
an arrow, split on the edge of a comet, into flame.

The woman in the gallery fell to the thresher's floor.
She lay at his feet in the whispering muds, the pomegranate
and wheat bright as ikon paints in the synagogue's
eternal dusk. She undid her hair and laid the Rabbi
out like the rule of life upon the pavement. He opened
his eyes and the Queen of Storm and Harvest set her foot
upon his brow. He rent his cloak and breathed in the
ghost-of-what-was-not.

The lion whelps in broad-brimmed, ermine hats, carried
him to the hillside and put him to rest in a blue stone box.

Until now, each year, on the day he died, the whelps come
and howl into their beards. The air near the tomb is
heavy with the sounds of the waters of life, herbs and the
dry light of the interior of the ark. Behind the
screen in the women's gallery a hag with yellow braids
watches the door, the blue grave and the eyes of the
lion whelps for the return of the lion and the
forms-of-those-things-that-yet-are-not-but-are-to-come.

The Donkey

The Donkey who is in the field
in this increasing fall is
tall as a hedge of wild rose.
He seals our dreams with grace:
a deliverance from rage
and intolerance of animals.
He is the gift of fallen apples
and rows of corn and ravens.
The dumb hoof of our blood
heaves on the barbed green.
He trots upon the sun. The horizon
brays through the orchard. His eyes
have seen the frost but
he burns with spring and Cici's hands
like links of crocus around his neck.

The Eden of the Vegetables

I am apple. You are pear.
They are weeds. Those, herbs.
The others, beans of various sorts.
Around the corner, the crowd:
cucumbers, onions, tiger lilies,
radishes and wild garlic. The rabble,
above the lawn on the stone terrace:
berries, asparagus, dandelions and
morning glories. We hang on our branches,
you Lady Pear, I Sir Apple. The world
rests, a cabbage too large for eating,
in the garden of days. The worm, beetle
and slug hover about, hissing and slicing
away at sap. The grass watches.
In the distance the sound of metal drives
through the loam and aloft in the toting
shadows: pruning sticks, torches, ladders, and the jam pot.

from

The Flag
the Hawk Flies

1972

Color

Blue is the stammerer's color.
Yellow, the color of the lion tamer.
Red, the signum of the clown.
White is the flag the hawk flies.
Orange, the kingdom's staff.
Green, the water bug's legs on the bank.
Black is the father's dream.
Rose, the candle-maker's, purple, the jeweler's colors.
Ochre, the potter's wrist.
Lapis, for the seated knight.
Opal, the bear.
Burnt sienna, the plowman's hood.
Cobalt, the color of the horse asleep.

Peridot is the color of the steeple jack.
Olive is the wind over the steeple.
Wasp green, what the steeplejack sees sprout from the timber of his fall.

Dun is what the rain turns over in the grave.
Turquoise, the color of a toad's death.

The garnet is the color of the trumpeter.

The color of blood is no color for in the ground
it turns like a bullet toward the root of wheat
and drives through snakes and seed
to rise up like breath in the simple grass.

The Horse

I am the horse that built the way
to the willow grove. Roots kick at
my hoofs. No flower still. I sway
through the corn like a judge.

This day I took him to a hollow.
Early it was. Just dawn. The
mist in the stall around my eyes. A fallow
time to dream the last horror.

He woke me with a slap on my rump.
I neighed the frost down from
my mane. The lump

of salt in my feed box like a
marble step on a holy stair
slides along my tongue. Start a
high day by backing smartly

from the stall. I do. And stand
head licking the air as he
throws tack upon my back. A grand
bit of leather too, shined

like amber, spurs and bit cold
but warmer than my hide pushing
against me with a silver bold-
ness that sends me stamping

on the floor. He led me to the road,
down to Skunk Hollow Lane,
mounted me, drove his heels in. Load
of him on my back and the morning

stirred wildness through me. I laid
out the way to the willow grove
and stopped there in my canter. Made
the morning was: sun up over the

Griggs' barn. Cows moving out to the field
the last day before their winter
hermitage. The dust settled from my

road. The gold oak; the red maple.
A wind from the wood carrying nuts,
frogcalls and logs and mushrooms full
of summer death. He shouted

in my ear. "Look, look, beast, a lake,
a lake there in the hollow. A mile long."
He leapt off. I smiled. No lake. A fakery
of morning. But he ran down to the shore

expecting whales. But there he saw just
a puddle. I'd done it with the morning light.
"Ah," he cried to me, "No lake." The crust
of day broke. He saw it for what it was.

Nine Prayers to the Trinity, to be Sung by the Nuns of Regina Laudis at Matins

God the Creator who made whales
and Jesus our Brother who wept
and ate bread
and the Spirit
who sprung the latch upon this birdsong
listen

God the Father who draws up
the wheat
and Jesus our Brother who
climbed mountains
and the Spirit
the plank they tread
listen

God the Builder of the sun
and Jesus our Brother who slept
through the night
and the Spirit
who thinks on the sea currents
listen

God the Father who halved
the void
into light and dark
and Jesus our Brother
who went to the well for water
and the Spirit who

holds the poles
apart
listen

Father of the bulls' horns
and the ribs of sharks
and Jesus our Brother who loved
deserts
and the Spirit
who plants roots in frost
listen

God the Maker of the wrist
of Bach
and Jesus our Brother who loved
fishnets
and the catch
and the Spirit who hungers
for the clocks
in snails
listen

God the Master who makes
the emerald
savor of the sky
and Jesus our Brother who
bit down on wood
and the Spirit who
grows poppies near marigolds
listen

Father God who lames beggars
and hurts
the widow when she thinks

and Jesus our Brother
who forgives the tides
their burial of corn
and the Spirit who remembers nothing
but the morning
listen

Father who dropped the seeds
into the mud
and let the green bark
dwell with the sloth
in Adam's wood
and Jesus our Brother
a sail upon the waves
and the Spirit
the birdsong
listen

On Reform

If they did not live you mean they did
not own a coat or shoe buckle nor answer
to a call: Respicious, Numpha,
Felix of Valois, Bacchus, Symphorosa.
That at night they did not turn down
the sheets and crawl into bed with wife
or child and rise up in the morning
to hear the lions roar in the dens beside
the river. If you name me am I then alive?
If you un-name me do I die and break the
flowerpot set above my tomb? When
the Lord comes to bring me to my bones
from days amidst the unflawed anemones
will I find my master blind to all I died
so gory for and hear him decree me null
and void and never was?
                                  Do Catherine, knuckled
on her wheel, Christopher, knee deep in mud,
Valentine and his mating birds, Placcid
and Ursula, their followers and their dreams
of Paradise stand alone now in the marble shadows,
their chapels burned, their statues rendered
into forks and spoons? But, I think,
like Aeneas, Hamlet, and Antigone they storm
the earth still, even as they fall, and sing
again, stronger than before, their blooded,
emblazoned, ruined prayers and swerve
closer to the face they felt in the lions' teeth.

The Mud Bird

She brushed off the dust that settled on the rolls
of raisins and hazelnuts. She lit the candle
in the window and called her child to supper.
The upper room was ready for the night; she
had folded back the cotton sheets and opened
the green tin box that held the bones from Sinai.
The sun snapped in the top branches of the tamarisk tree.
In the kitchen the porridge thickened in the bowl.
She called her child again to table but he played
in the mud at the end of the street and did not
answer. He'd seen a rose in the morning
and wished to make it fly when the leaves
moved and the thorns cast acid shadows on the bricks
the rose vine climbed upon. He pressed a bird
from the mud and held it in his hands like pollen
drifting on the tongue of a bee. He shattered a speckled
stone and pressed in the fragments where the wings
would be and waves of blood curved over
the earth and ran into the mud. Dead fish
in the oven saw a shoal of claws come up
from the fire. The child pulled the mud out
to the edge of a feather and peered into the breast
and whispered: "You are a bird, fly." It lifted up
its belly from the ground, fluttered its wings,
but could not mount the air. The child looked again
within the bird and said:"Fly, I am Jesus.
Build a nest in the top branches of that tamarisk tree."
The mud bird laid his head in the dust.
His beak curled and black feathers
fell like scorched fans upon the ground.

His mother stood beside the child and said:
"But boy he has no name. You may be God
but it will not hear you if you do not name him."

The boy bent over the void the mud bird
had summoned from the earth (life is terrible
for a creature in the hands of gods) and called out,
"Robin, Robin, Robin." It leapt into the sky and touched
the child with the shadow of its wings
and the last mud from its airy claws.

A Philosophy

In the world we know one thing
and one thing only: that love is
not easy and likely to trouble dreams,
turn the mind onto droughts
and the end of hope. In this world
we find the one we seek
and then would drive it out
as if it were a fog under the door
threatening the hearth.
It was always so. Penelope
felt the loom warp; the oak
breaks into crimson and the green
sands on the bottom of the turtle pond
suck in the lily. Let it be
so: if a philosopher would find
the sorcery to end all strife
in love, banish him.
If a face, summoned from the mud,
is doric in the brow and if, when the fire
settles in the nostril and the light fits into the space
between the eyes the sound is a
door opening toward a drumming
in the trees, then leave the room
and spend the day away from windows
and mirrors for that loved face
comes again and again and will not
stop coming when you banish it.
This is certain too: you cannot
banish body from the body; that
is what love is at the beginning of love—
the body and just the body. If
you would have it other, leave this world

and live upon a leaf in an Indian sky.
So. There is nothing for us then but love.
It is man's way in life. To love
and then not to love. It is so and it will be
until the end of love; until the body's end.

The Metaphysician

The nave of the syllable is uttered. The belltower
echoes the syllable and the clerestory bolts
the syllable to the keystone in the portal where
the virgin and the saints spin through their rigid glory.

The rose windows drift in the moss and vines of the outer walls.

The metaphysician neighs being to the spiders in the apse.

Thus it rings: truth, touched by fire and light;
object in water; orange on a table; child with hoop
at his heel; dust on a silver dish; these objects
in their altitudes and spheres of shadow.

The bulk and heft of its periods: shells, kelp, wooden spools,
pink skeleton of crabs and tracks of sea wren impale the surf;
the word rests on the strand of the text;
ivory ladders of signs, burnished verbs, waterfalls of adjectives,
and the senses nailed to the margins, blue and yellow as eagles and waves.

In the hollow of the hillside, honeycombs and barrels of clover wine
spill in the winds that lie athwart the fields of Silbury in view
of the sacred mound on the Way of Mwnhir where fern and grazing cattle
blacken out the sun. Branches of bees and flowering nuts spin
in the cleft of being where metaphysician utters the syllable:
OPHIR ENS AMPHEE ELI ARBIME EUREKA

Sandcastle

When the sea comes up out of the deep sands
the sandcastle built with that sand is best.
The walls are firmer, the turrets and moats
stand against the battering of the seasons in the waves.
Build a wall with the sand on shore
and it falls after the sun warms it.
Not so with the deep sands: those are sands
that see no light, no parasol. No gulls' eyes
watch them. The dark sands. The volcanic ones
that never breathe wild rose scent.
The sullen sands.

The Resurrection Day
of a Brown Bear

It was not the same, not precisely
as it had been, but like enough
to make the resurgence of bulked and battering
flesh a charm. Where he'd been all the years
since the lake caved in and he'd sunk
without a sound to the blooming rockbed
of the arctic he did not wish to think about.
He'd some uneasy thoughts about a window
and a blue field but no dream or memory
of the bear he was and life for him without
the bear in him was not life at all.
He'd been called Arroyo and he'd held the hills
near Compostela in his arms. The hills were
his will. He had leaned on every violet
hay stack and apple and no child or lady, shepherd
or bishop in his frock dared go about the land
until they'd knocked on wood and called his name
three times against the light to banish fear.
He was a princeling, descended from a unicorn
and a polar bear. When he had grown old he traveled
north until the arctic circle moved beneath him.
He spent the days tramping on the ice, kicking over
mounds of ancient snow, frozen butterflies and moths
fell like slivers of Sumerian lintels on the heaving
crown of the world.
                    Now 500 years gone by
he feels the sinew and blood begin to blister
along the bone. The rubble of his dust takes on weight
and fur picks out the lines around his eyes. He is
too large for the fathoms of his grave and soon

his paws, his neck, his hip and belly push aside
the ice and frozen wheats and he stands up full
height beneath the waters that on his resurrection day
grow warm and light as pollen. He rises up. When he
puts his head above the surface of the sea he knows
it all again: the violets, the pilgrims on the way
to Compostela, the wail of the wood cock on his tongue
and the herbs and spells of the hills. And starved
from centuries without flesh and blood he pounces on
a singing carriage of novices and their guardians and gulps
them down as if he'd never touched a living thing before.

To Sister Ann
on the Occasion of Her Being
a Nun for One Day

On the first night, a virgin's eyes, once
set upon by her husband's body
in its holy terror, shift like
glass in a kaleidoscope and take on
new dwelling places of light.

Now Christ shines through the linen
boards of your wimple in the warm hearth
of your will, true as any buck
his dreams cast off.

             Like a plate
fallen from a mantle when an earthquake
rocked the keystone you have seen the
beginning of all love, breached
by such an one as he who made the world.

Drunk on the Lord's Wine

Such drunkenness! The priest had filled
the chalice to the brim and when he took
a sip and the friends around the table
their delicious portion, the chalice came
to me half full of the Lord's earthy blood.
I drank it down in two gulps. It ran like
buds of wisdom in my throat. I'd not eaten
all the day, till the plate of God's bread,
but for an orange in the morning. Suddenly
the wisdom I had swallowed built a trellis
round my flesh and weighed me down with plow,
shears, trundle and ladder of the harvest.
I swayed in my chair. I stood and sat quickly
down again. The floor had leaned against me.
The window rolled from its frame and closed
round my skull. I was drunk on the Lord in a
bright tide of a sensual spell.

                    Well, there I was
six floors up in the middle of a block I knew but
did not know for I was drunk on the Lord's
blood and such a drunkenness it was.

The Eagle

That eagle knew iron distances.
No full traps. Hills cracked
by the newborn ice whipped on
the sun's rim, spelled him. His
feathers turned heavy with the
plummeting earth. At the center
of a curve in the miles of his
desolation, he saw, that morning,
the Norseman walk out of his pelt
hut, hitch up his britches with a
leather belt (the buckle, copper,
two jaws of a stunned deer in flight
joined in blunt shriek at his belly)
and kicked aside a crystal lump
between tracks of a wild shadow,
and snapped his fingers. The eagle
watched from his hot branch.
"Come brotherhood, scatter from
the thickets and gnaw my bones.
O this pelt world and its inky heat."
(Then there was one man and one eagle
in the transparent orb of the world's
brain.) "If there be others, come,
enchant, kill, speak and fall asleep
with me in the darkness of my thigh."
(We infer the desert not from the ant
with the dozen red eyes huddled in
the rift between strokes of wind but
from the drift of the pear tree in
the dark. The desert is everywhere,
most certainly just as fullness comes.)
On its hot branch, weighed down with

the hunger of the plain, the eagle crouched
in the man and man in the eagle, drifting,
above, beneath each other, like flowers
aloft. The eagle descended from branch
to branch until it stood uncertain as a
boat on a barn floor, on the earth.
The world lay about them unconsumed,
like a dish of wine in a beggar's dream.
There was a truce of blood, a strength,
of flesh and a gentleness of light when
that man bent, like a green branch
into a pool, in the eagle's eyes.

When I Would Love
and Cannot Love

When I would love and cannot love
then I know the rules of love
that render me complete and still.

In this new age redeemed by love,
I cannot dream of love and not awake
and dream of love again
even as I know that dream will
go when this new age,
redeemed by thunder from the fields, is still.

I am not of this opinion
held by some I love
that love is a fit of nerves
and vanishes, if it is ill begotten
in the world, like thunder into barns
where the fields are sundered
from the rocks. I have this opinion:
love a cubit adds to my depth
and height and cannot go from me.

I have said, once when there seemed
just this exquisite joy
followed by another and then another
that love was this and

nothing other but then I learned
that this love was each day
renewed
as the thunder comes through
the ceiling when the storm is gone.

from

How to Put Out Out
a Fire

1984

I Bronzi Di Riace:
Threnody for a Poet Who Died
After She Had Seen Them

Their grappling hooks had found your lips.
I Bronzi in their diving gear snared
your ankles, upending you in the sand.
Cocks in brine, thighs like plates of jade,
these roustabouts in the sea's suck and pity
poured their skin over your breasts;
the corroding tides salt jaw tucked
back your joints. You loved their hulk,
these victors over the electric eel and
the garrulous man-o-war, Medusa, who eats
like breathing. Your men: calamitous, marginal beaux.

At the fundament of the drowned flame,
where is the sill sublime, the candle
of the forge, the sail of Vulcan,
the sea top is ripped, the sac, erupt,
your caved-in heart is gobbled down. *I
Bronzi di Riace* bend toward your nipples, lift
you up upon their backs and in a cascade of
clattering muscle and groping limbs float you into paradise.

The Cave

It is a four hour walk from Montaillou
over rocks and dry riverbeds,
through scorpion nest and briar hedge,
up hillsides where earth lies like mange
upon the eyes, to the cave. The sun throws
its belly on the trees and turns them
into lapses of midsummer, burning them flat.
Black feathers hang on the branches
of those trees where vultures had keeled
over in the pan of light. In the distance
the cave fretted in the clotted air
and a boiling midday pain lapped
around me without patience.

On my hip I carry, in a leather
pouch, within an enamel box, wrapped
in linen, God's body. Jammed in
beside him, a toothbrush, matches,
soap and in a knapsack, tins of vegetables,
a pot of honey, pad, pencil, a bible,
flashlight and a pallet of cotton
sniffed in corduroy.
I will spend one month alone
within this cave to catch the demons
in the imperial climates of my flesh.

The first night I slept soundly until
the morning sun spilled upon the stone
and its warmth reached through to my skin.
I heated a pan of water, made tea,
put honey on a slab of bread
and took them out onto the ledge and sat

looking down upon the valley. Morning
moved like a tide of weeds toward noon.
On the fifth day the sun seemed
like a glaze of ice upon my cheeks.
A herd of cattle without a herder
were caught on the plain. They shifted
their grazing toward the cordillera
their way toward a river
that gawked like a walleye in the shadows.
The day hung on me, a stiff cloak of the mold
of air. I feared a snake would
garrote me as I slept.
I buried a candle in the dirt. It
burned away into the earth and a snake
sidled into my dream and stretched
itself across my eyes.

One whom I thought was the crested
plenum of desire leaned upon me
as I slept. Ah my troubled hair,
my thighs railed against, my neck
fretted with kisses, in my mouth
the trumpet of tongues.

When I awoke the enamel box above me
had fallen upon the floor.
The bread within tipped out
lying like a shell of light
sprung from the sun's delirium.
I crouched before him. Then
it was as if I had not known
the river flowing through my childhood,
nor had ever seen the hair on my belly,
as if I could not write my name,

or belt my cassock, as though
I had not heard the spoken colors
of birds or had watched the herd
stumble over the plain, nor ever
gathered up the water from the
farmyard well. I watched the
bread and would swear even now, long
afterward as I tend the pigs and meet
the crested plenum of desire in the
cloister as I sweep the cobwebs from
the beams, that it uttered, as if
grain and yeast had taken up the
language of the fields, a word to me.
He spoke in my tongue and said
"*Enfin.*" I looked down into
the valley. The cattle had found
their herder who gathered them
into his body. They trekked to
the river. They drank of it and in
bantering lights, in the mulled air,
I heard the word again, small as a hornet
swivel across my brow and thought,
Yes, Lord, *enfin.*

Some Thoughts of a Monk in the Cloister of Vietri Sul Mar

You said: it is time to lie down together
and watch the nude light from the sea skim
through the shutters. We lay down. Then
you said: watch the shadows on the far wall.
I did. Your hand moving in arcs above
your head played like smoke upon the white walls.
Then I said: The light on your face, in the shade
of the great leaf of the sun is heavy
with my blood. Your brow is narrow, not grand.
I must touch it lest the thing I built from
passion I see passion kill. I touch your skin,
flee the spirit's harder dimes. Better
roam the ramps and buttresses of your legs
and back than greet you in the soul's garden.

May I tell you that I love you still?
I love your name and in the dark light
of dusk, in the copper light of evening,
in the underside of light that lights
my dreams, I fold myself about thee like
a tree 'round the green column of air that is
its copious habitat. Now, when the vistas
of your soul's garden open, as the shutters do
when the winds hurt the rusted metal hinges, I
touch your palm that turns upward like a plate.
Through the porcelain surface of the evening
sea you shine upon me nude as water.

Peace, after Long Madness

After a long madness peace is an assassin
in the heart. Where there had been the clenched
fist, the strung out sinew, the hamstrung grin,
the erect eye and hand on every shadow like a spy,
now the river springs from the crystal of its sleep
in a sapphire lunge to the sea. A year of madness
is a libation poured out of nettles and boiled
herbs, of knives oiled with honey that cut silently
to the spine. I was madness's kin, no, more its
parent blood, its coursing lymph, its skeleton.
I kept company with lunacy, broke bread with him,
lay beside him, my head in his arms, felt him draw
down the sheet to watch me as I shook and so it was
one year till now.
                    Now the rocks become a sweetness
in the listless meadow, the lutist brays to
the ashes, flowers in the red crystal bowl push
against the windowpane and I sleep again,
my hands beneath my cheek, legs straight out,
eyes shut against the inward stratagem of dream
and the bedsheets and counterpane lie upon me
no more leaded capes of knobbed steel, but companions
of my skin, like the surface of my river is kindred
balm to the volcanoes and riven headlands that lie beneath it like pain.

Biting Down on Fish

Fish is always fish.
Not like meat that
has no link after roasting
to its animal: beef, not cow,
pork, not pig, but fish—
fish. Bite down on fish and
taste the dry beast who
takes water in like
sand on a hoop.
I have never thought of fish as wet.
Had trout
and octopus
and finished off some two dozen
or more small fish lured
by bread into a pail
and then spilt into a vat of boiling
olive oil.
I bit down on those, through
eye, brain, chest,
small as a dot on a sun flash
as the oil floated
the small stink of death like
the air round a thistle
floats the thorn.

This Alchemy

I rest my hand upon you
like a hornet on a bramble.
You are the blush of light
on my heart.
My bed is still. The floor
lies like a knife. The walls
teem with the sounds of cupidons
raging at puppets in heat.
The doors lean on the shadows.
Between your arms I lay my
body, the monster of my innerlife
candled like a leaf of sighs
within your sumptuous walls of skin.

Examinations into the Maniacal Self

I.

He is a gigantic elf entrapped in his immensity
He sits on plankton.
Inkling of wings in the bantering of his hoofs
even as he sleeps.
Taking off through the underbrush
he leers at the light
as if he himself were the limit of eternity.
He cannot know
how nothing sleeps when he does.
His dreams are not tactful.
For instance in one he chumped off his own head
at the drop of his wife's shoe.

II.

Frater Loon, I was afloat on the middle kingdom
of lust, half bird, half man, no habitation in cell
or in cliff grass, a bare-assed wreck
hankering after you who'd fixed a ring to his nose
and fled to spoils of diligence.

III.

Frater Gerbil in his coffee can pecks at the light
with his nose, aloft on the windowsill.
He roasted there one day when I left him
on my trip to grocer and flower shop.
I knew his agony, burning with a fire he could not shuck.

IV.

Frater Chrysanthemum, I bought you on a green
morning and then you died. I tended you with

water, light and pruning and then one day
in the snow and fire of a great storm you came alive
again, green buds bucking out of dry stems.
I knew it all too well, the dry dazzle and birth
of love, then the nicked blood, the lean, boned
hillside, the ashes of blizzards and the copper glory
cupping the off pitch root in its bole.

V.

I built the Chinese Wall, now tumbled down, to
keep gerbil, loon and chrysanthemum from the farside of
my ribboned hat: the safe isles through inferno,
the silver combs and double mirrors of reflection,
the groomed staff were of no avail. The bugle
spring of your lip, the dumb wail of this thin bed
filled all of space with one body. I would not be this wreck
but I am and it is my glory Amen.

A Journey

I.

I stood against the wall of your flesh
and yelped with hope that this was the holy
bonding that would loose the ash in
the ornamental trees and the seed pods
in the dry rock pools that they might swarm
with decoration. My freed blood roamed
my sinew and brain like tar afire.

II.

On the currents of my crabbed blood
I walked toward you like Eros split with rue.

III.

Amish ladies cannot quilt bright colors
in the solitude of their rigid parlors
but quilt in guarded kinship with other
ladies. This quilt, bright red triangles
and white was thought perhaps a heater
of the blood, firing pin of the rested
nipple. Amish ladies would come out
of hiding to watch me cast off their quilt
as I discover your creature body,
shape neither white triangle nor red
in this sewing room where thy flesh and mine
is scalloped, hemmed, pulled tight, patterned.

IV.

Anemones, crows, wild rose, in the fleece
of salt caught in the air from the sea beyond
the marshes, each doric pitch of stone,
had turned, in the ruby lymph of the scorched
sea's radiant face to fluted discs of flame.

(We had feasted there in Paestum on a bowl
of mushrooms and pasta in a sauce of herbs
and garlic with wine from the neighbor hills;
napkins white and damp, hemmed with green thread.)

But that light fell, when I turned to tell you
it had come, headlong into the fields as if oxen
harnessed with ice had thudded against the sun.

V.

The light on your face is sweet,
that rabid light that tolls
in my soul's garden like Eros'
idiot child.

VI.

The Amish quilt lies
like a sail upon your
body. I search the wind
to move that sail but
no wind comes from anywhere.

O that I might turn into
that wind and move that sail,
to be thy craft again,
thy body's bellied spinnaker.

A Dream: Barrington Rhode Island

I knew you lived in that room: the polished floors,
the chests gleaming like lacquers, the door
knobs hung each with a silver tassel. Chairs and tables
placed like votive chattel. Each gable
of light cupped like a nerve about the walls.

Noon cracked. I stood erect. Your thigh stalled
upon the lintel. I held fast. Covered my head
with my hands. You crossed my brow like a straw reed.
The floors thundered.
                When I looked up I saw a child
standing beside me. I said: "It is a lovely day, mild
as hayfields, so gentle." The child touched me on
my cheek and smiled. "It is so because I am here."

I woke in this room. Scanned the walls. The moon
was up. The sea pruned the morning from the reefs.
The clock, heavy with chimes of salt, tolled through the sheets.

How to Put Out a Fire

All day long and unto night sacrificial fire is kept burning.
Dawn brightens and the altar shows no trace of ashes, no
fragments of half burned logs—but is covered with dew and
fresh grass which comes up again every night.

—ANELIAN, N.A. 1050

I.

Remove from the field all tinder:
nettles, the straw clown, the paper
fan, the old man's yawn, the kite,
the mauve dalliance in the shadow.
For the shade will not be pierced
with runnels from the sun, no matter
how the clay strums for the potter's
fire. The hedge will not trip the brimstone in the din.

II.

The nipples: store them in vinegar.
For the belly: cords of barbed wire.
For calves and thighs: masks of corduroy.
For the breasts: bars of bass notes.

III.

The eyes are the hottest fields.
No carpet of furnaces nor planks of steaming
jars of oil can rival the eye in its
candling of flesh. Light holds up
the spine, the heel and toe into locks
of the seraphic blood.

IV.

So we must put out our fire and gouge the flint,
reduce the corruscating rest in the blood
to ice. We must pull up the root that flares
its volcanic leaf and lower into vats of rocks
and lizards the rested mouth and the small ramp
of muscle that connects the hip to the inner leg:
reduce then, to brazen chill the esplanades
and covenants of flesh and the coursing dream
that claps for consummation.

The English Poet's French Lover

It was agreed that she would not
wear veils nor color her nails red.

There would be always a cousin in
attendance. The alcove in the den, the bed,

the supper hour, the walk in the garden,
the late night cheese and wine—instead

of toils of speculation there would be
cries of music uttered aloud, led

by a court of scribes in green
caps, khaki britches and a mode of lead

about their eyes. In early morning,
when the shades were still down, the tread

of feet unslippered could be heard in the attic
where the poet and his lover fled

from the scrutiny of collapsed syllables
and crushed verbs to rush head on

toward the pubic arch and its apocalyptic glades.

The Bather

I slept with her like a hawser in my arms.
(I watched her like a bat cooped in a glut of vine.)

She rolled about the bed like a clown in heat.
(I touched her like a smithy's tongs pluck the sizzling nail.)

I kissed her like the mouse, the cheese on the baited spring.
(She cracked her fingers on my skull like jets of pins.)

I woke with her like a bagpipe on my chest.
(She leapt from bed and pulled the plug from night.)

She dressed in the robes of morning like a drone of wills.
(And cupped each toe to paint it red and whisked it with her palm.)

She ate her bread with suet on a shard of tile.
(And walked naked to the swiveling sands.)

Sailboats tacked about her, a fleshy beacon, a swollen weed.
(She spread her legs and pissed into the sea.) Some bathers

saw her and hid behind the rocks; she was immense.
(Steam rose from where she wet the tide.)

A fisherman, a smithy and a gatherer of flax remembered her.
(The next day fire struck the flaxen harvest, a stallion

turned the forge over on the smithy's hands and bells tolled
where the fishnets lay await for morning) and the bell rope

spun round its iron wheel and pressure of clanging made
babes deaf, closed the jaws of gulls and glazed

the light with a slime so dense there were no seasons for a year.
(And in that night I slept with her like a hawser in my arms.)

New Poems

Panther

When the panther came
no belfrey rang alarums,
no cleric spat his tea.
When the panther came
the sky and lawn were still.
The panther came
through forest,
through field,
up to the wall
and my one blossoming cherry tree.

I had constructed
the world as it was
and had pared the body
from customs of languor.
It pressed its nose against
the pane and its gears
ground me away into ribbons
of dissonance.

It turned and sauntered
into the shadows. Its
paw marks on the earth
like cherries too ripe in a white bowl.

Sitting There

Sitting there before the sun,
cutting into it,
leaning into it,
putting one toe,
then the foot,
into it,
its waves of contour
and explosion,
letting it curl up
the belly,
lipping it all the way
to the neck,
jaw, lips, nose
and finally to the eyes.
Looked into it,
the beckoning fish
and the cat,
scratching at bales
of fire.

The Vessel of Light

This valley:
nettles,
scorpions,
tiny jaws of crickets,
the wild boar's spoor,
the torrent,
will snare light
at the end of the sun's
fleshed illuminations.
It falls
on the hard earth:
boiled shards,
the blooded rim,
the plaque
of the sweet garlic
sweat of all
the gods and slow
as honey on a peak
of ice, it runs
into the earth
its will breathless
as young girls
swimming upstream
against desire.

When the resplendent
chords of dawn
crank up the world
the light reels in
and there it floats,
the air,
like a glittering fish

caught by the girls swimming upstream
and turned round
by day and
the beginning
of the sun's finny
descent toward
the torrent,
the wild boar's spoor,
scorpions,
and the tiny jaws
of crickets.

This Great Vat of Sense

Where is the entrance to the soul?
The body cannot be unto itself,
apart, against the skin, and pine
for solitude like tides for monuments.

The world in its sweeps and dives of
cranium, in the doped highlands, on
deadwalls, in the decay of leaves,
in air tangled with salt, in this great

vat of sense, mounts the nose,
for the nose is the entrance to the soul.
Manure, the septic log, the lizard
spinning on the hot fat of noon, cheese

carnivorous with rot, rosemary on the hands,
peel away the ambiguities within the
body's shell and spill into the soul
to the first layer, then to the

seventieth, coursing finally to the
chicken, black with cognac, who lifts
its gutted eye and sniffs the shadow
of man as if he were a hatchet.

States of Mind

I. THE AUTISTIC

In the wetlands of sound
I have set up my camp.
my mind is brackish. Words
too long in the hollow stone
of my brain have floated
up round my face and hold me
in an aquatic stall: like the
winter time of bees in a hive of ice,
the queen bolted to an icicle,
her subalterns, their wings
shining, honey on the filaments,
caught in a cantilevered
spasm of the abysmal now.

II. THE MAP

He had caught it, the curve
of the river and the landing,
the barge and then the river
gone round the cliff. He
raced to write it down and saw
it rush over the boulders into a gully
and bash into a forest. Lost it,
but got it: the lines of it,
the little cube he drew
into the shoreline to explain
just what the map was a picture of
and why he'd do no more of this
but let it go and not record another wandering inch.

III. THE POET

He just let it end. He had
looked into the windows
of the sun and
needed then to break
them open with his body
as he had the body of his
beloved but
he was broken by that leap and
could not undo the scorching.

Objets de la vie de tous les jours

This double almond will be used against convulsions
and this amber bracelet against the lethargy
after some many flagons of wine. This laurel against heresy
and this print of a lizard against time.

This caliper against the toothache. This basket
against the will and this sieve against
the noonday sun. This rake against birth and this
bird in obsidian against thy lover and his stun.

This oven against thirst and this empty bottle
against the river at my feet. This mourning
cloth against death, this cup of burnt grain
against the plague and the red salamander in your breath.

This ripe tomato against the snap of the dry earth
and this drowned scorpion against the shadow
and this emergence of blood from the womb.
This hammer against wayfaring lightning and the builders of your tomb.

Fulco di Verdura: A Vanity

Petrified by a fiery testament
crystals piled one atop another
in a jagged pile are a flamboyance.
Lian de Pougy cracked one with
her teeth. Demoiselle Orlandi hung
two about her neck on a lapis hook.
Mathilde de Morny tucked one between
her lover's legs. Paquerette held
slivers in Picasso's paint box.
Caryathis set hers on a dish
between two ripe tomatoes.
They exhaled a crystal breath
that cooled poppies and stopped
rains from entering wells.
When they walked moons
stumbled into tides
and streets fell into manholes.

Then di Verdura came and gathered
them into his pestle
and from the flotsam tooled a brace
of high-cooked mica dolphins,
twisted them into manacles
and bound the hands and lacquered
ankles of all the fairies in the Bois de Boulogne.

Tulips

They are very still in jars,
in pots, in garden beds; they
are very still. The wind slides
by them, leaving the air clamped
down by their stems like jade poles;
their leaves like elephant ears.
The other garden flowers plod through
their roots toward the floated rivers
that undercut the walls and benches
of the paths that bleed the lawns to civil fields.
Tulips, thin girls, bonneted, in the straight
pattern of virginity, cackle (though mute
as spines) in the avenue where the arbor stills the heart.

The Eyes of Shetland Ponies

I had seen thunder clouds gathered
over Stonegrave, chomping the skies,
a platter of ebony axes, just off
chaos, ready to drop.

These animals mulled about a
tumulus, pulling roots and turf
from a savage skull. In the
corner of their eyes two men

walked with a dog. It was a
musky day; the mist was the sea
upon which floated the ambergris
of their thought in a sac

of sub-tonic fiddlings. The
odor of passion angered these
ponies and they massed together
and cornered them against

a fence. From the fields and ponds
stuffed with spores came the scent
of mallow, grape hyacinth, beaver,
the aboreal kangaroos and rose moscheta.

Ram

He holds the field between his horns
and earth curls round his hoofs.
His eyes look at nothing, yet he sees
divinity's crooked fingers
scratching the meadow. The worm
shunts aside, and moles, butterflies
and floating eagle flee the sinewy
terror of his spotlight eyes.
"Now, listen," the sky says, "it is
yours, this expanse of whispers
and distances." The bickering wife
in the house stops her clatter at
the chopping board and parts the curtains,
peers into the field where Ram,
stud of the clover, couples with his dame,
chomping on her fleece, a fearful thing,
this four-footed intercourse on the hot
bolster of midsummer.

She Had Seen It First in the Sky

A huge swarm of dangerous African bees flew across the field
above the cricketers' heads and briefly caused everyone to lie
flat on the ground.   —HARARE, SOUTH AFRICA, 1990

She had seen it first in the sky,
a distant confusion, and tilted her parasol
away from the sun to see it clearer.
The players, in the white perspective
on the green field, clothed against
the heat in loose flannel, constructed
the horizon so that it quivered, a line
of convulsed light on the cornea, as if a
honeycomb had fallen into a whirlwind.

She had heard it first in the sky,
a proximate confusion, and tilted her parasol
away from the sun to hear it better.
The players in the white perspective
on the green field, clothed against
the heat in loose flannel, tilted
the horizon so that it leaked black
torpor as if a jungle had stepped
onto a grief-stricken lawn.

She saw it clear, cropping the willows,
caloric pebbles, a present damage on the air,
and tilted her parasol away from the setting
sun to see it clearer. The players in
the white perspective of the green field
looked up into the funnel of reverberation
and heard it come, a separate carillon,
aspersions of fire, and when it kissed
the pitch they fell upon the grass

———

and looked up into the underbellies
of a swarm of killer bees and the white
perspective, belly down in the grass,
bat and ball scattered like sea wrack.
She tilted her parasol down to
cover the field for she would not
bear the weight of it, sun, the bees,
the world unforeshortened, as all things go
to the uttered curve of pain.

Rubens Peale's Glasses

Descending toward his hair, toward the light
on his forehead, toward the pleated shield
of silk at his throat, the geranium plant
with luminous speed coils round my parsimonious
inner life. His right hand on the edge
of the pot, two pairs of glasses, one
beneath his palm, the other on the bridge
of his nose. Oh young Rubens Peale
what do you see that you could not see
through the other lens? Was it the
"lifted sea" upon the petals, the curl of
blood swaggering round the red pot's molding
or the barbarous, sensuous blight of plant
life moving toward you, solemn botanies,
grains of dry light, the shift upon your
lips of the spindrifts of amplitude?

Three Poems for Jane Howe of Red Horse Farm

ALEXANDER

When he had got the curl right,
just above his left brow
and untied his blouse
so the ruddy hair lay across
the boy's eyes
like a ladder
he snapped about
and said:
"Slide down my spine
and smell
the battle in the pores,
nestle your mouth
on my thigh
where Persian javelins
breathe in me
like collected bee stings.
Follow me into the wood
of the black columns
where birds wander off
and snap the heads
of violet and grape.
Pass your hands there
below my throat
where the watched night glistens."
But fixed in his head
like a shelf of clocks
were the battles
to be fought.

He had been caught off balance
by the marshes beyond
the river, smirking
like burned mouths
and the junk yards there of armor
and flesh.
The tight halter of his mind
looked down upon the head that had
fallen on his chest
flicking lashes on his bones.
Prisms of space crunched
the light around him,
ludicrous thing
with the diadems of all the world
scalding his brain.

CONES OF THE CEDAR OF LEBANON

Whatever not here clearly observed
is, in the cones of the Cedar of Lebanon,
outside your window
where the seasons are in their
encumbered certainty
exemplars
of the passage out.
As the sap dries, as the green
spittle of the cone
is caught in the casings of
overlapping larva, of this leaf
and that shadow
is it a consolation of sorts?
For the bone and blood,
companion heralds of light
are camouflage of the indentured
flesh. They are lamps on the mud paths,

turning, burning the grit
away so that, like the cones,
when they unfold, like a drained sun spot,
you will gather round you
luminescences
of the candled face
seeping through the light
now finally complete.

COOK

The cook said: when the revelation comes,
it comes: unpardonable error
in the yeast, the crust ringed
by fire balls, the pan restive
on the stove as if the oven were a fault
in the dough: its racks and levers,
dials and pilot light,
a cartographer's squint into
apocalypse. O yes it is
exactly that: the kitchen
hot or cold, seasons and seasons
forever.
The coals burn.
The iron is hot.
What could make it right?
Was the elbow too long in the dough?
The lemon too long in the rain forest?
What sent the steam up
the bottom of the pan,
through the greased surface
but could not save the bread
from the vines of mildew
and corruption in the zest?

Portrait of a Lady in Yellow

Alesso Baldovinetti (1426–1499)

Madame, turn
that I might
see your face
hidden in the shade
of the fan-light.
Lift me.
I am grown into
the stone
that divides me
from worldly ways
from benedictions,
from the coarse
philosophical bands
that go round and round.
Passion
crouches in the shadow
of the fan-light.
I am like
no other man.
I watch and when
you will turn and face me
whole and in your blazing
habiliment, I shall
be storm and gorging wave
and construe
from what you are
what I shall be
and again and again
to walk without
companion.

Poems upon Poems

Poems upon poems let there
    to lie under all the
fragrant doors and planks
    so long in the condor's
shadow. It is as if
    I had no time for even
treks through the snow
    or through the transformed
garden where I had remembered
    the colors of delphinium
and iris as if they were
    the passage of light
across my eyes. So they
    are there: the domain
underfoot, its assizes
    and its public executions
and wedding party winding
    through the hail and up
to its knees in mud.

Wittgenstein Reads *Finnegans Wake* in Provence: A Pauline Reflection

Take this stone, this word, this flower, this boy.
Take them or not. Set each down somewhere.
I look upward and see the nail that held the net.
Let each be. Each to its own pretension.
Alone. Then how long? Women will come surely:
The gloves, the creature with books, the sacrifice.
The net is no longer above me. The nail only.
I am distracted by the sun. It has folded
across the boy's back, swallowing him. The page
is hot. The boy, the flower, the stone, the word go up in flames.

Adopt a Visibility Sight

a sign on the road from Chatham to the Sagamore Bridge

You will never see it all from here.
"C'est noble." "C'est splendide." Albertine
de Montebello, leaning on the Sevres blue
handle of her cane was heard to declare
to the Chancelier de Fleur. (C'est splendide,
the acme of pride.) The lake, now cadmium
edged with red, spins in the air like, in its
texture, a raked, cobblestone esplanade
leading to the flowering waters of his waistcoat,
that hover on his chest as if it were the
underwing of a strelitza (violet turning to blue),
from the parting of your hair to your brow to
the top of your skull, in the maladroit
thigh . . . oh, all too, too beyond my theology . . .
I saw her but for an instant before they
brought down the coffin lid. I shoot my cuffs
and think of Verasis de Castiglione sitting
before her photographer, head tilted toward the
flash, flesh ruddy with the light for she had
never left her rooms and from all the beginnings
of days and nights she saw what she saw and
it sufficed until the lid came down and she
felt the satin plush brush her lips and shut them down too.

Poems on a State of Final Distraction

A heath and a desert in the going forth.
The dust of the Bent,
The Mezerion Tree
Strawberry leaves dying,
Burnt Wilde,
Flowers that perfume the air,
A little turrett with a belly.

    —FRANCIS BACON

I.

In the spindles of light
that winter trees do with the sun
air is shadow and bones of root
peer from the frost.

I am the gardener
of the mezzogiorno.
Summer words come through
the grime of slush,
through burnt arches,
for this is the light too
of thin calibrations.

I was out with black cotton
to give the birds "an uneasy limitation
of something not quite understood."
The wild parrot
gorged on Anna Pavord's
chubby Samuel Arnott and the common snowdrop.
"Strong secaturs" in hand I went
down "thrilling informal alleys"
where a mound of purple sprouting broccoli
lay shredded by rabbits
starved with seer berries and curds of straw.

———

I could no longer run it out.
I called to him through my teeth.

II.

White was the only possible colour.
—FROM A LETTER TO COUNTRY LIFE

The crepuscular stair
mounted the air
without nails: the illusion
of wood, a gasp of a landing
on a loop of wind,
that was it for him
as he rounded the door sill.
Beyond the shell
of the first step was a mantle
leaning against a pale, thin wall.
And on the mantle two birds of paradise
made of melted white sheets of water
that had come down from the hills
where the accompanying dereliction
had unloosed the rocks
that held back the floods of recollection.

He called to him through his teeth
who was not there.

III.

The Blushing Angel
—FROM AN ILLUMINATED MANUSCRIPT

When she had looked on God
she blushed and though no sex
had named her, she acted out
the girl and shut the glory out
with her lashes.

Sassetta in Vermont

Who is it that whispers so cold
in the flamboyant hedge and cuts
through the air like a hooligan?
What is it all about?
I see three larch a mile away
in the freeze, so clear
they seem like skeletons of fish
dangling from a hook in light.

Why it's Job on a rampage.

Sassetta on a sled comes roaring
down, splashing his ascetic
paints on the flat probe of winter
where every spent thing lacerates
the joints of feeling.

Aqueducts, pitfalls, conduits,
swollen roots,
the butterfly's severed
flight, all of nature consents to this
calamity, this lizard time,
this dry flower of oxygen and commits
an outrage on the land.

The sunshadows slip down into the earth,
the swivel of death's wan portal
pushes aside the hail that has fallen
across the passerby's eyes and
Job on a rampage, in a dervish moan,
descends upon the cloven day.

_____

She lifts a finger to her temple,
to the brittle vein,
pries it open and the gold in Sassetta's
paint box spills out into the bundled
wind and soul concludes
its golden age and, Job, his annunciation done.

The Photo Shoot

Piero della Francesca
Pala Montefeltro
Pinacoteca di Brera

I.

Where did they go after the Virgin
left with the child? And they were
alone with the egg hanging
from the contorted scallop shell.
Montefeltro, what did he do?
Go back to Gubbio and read another
book, sit on his illusion bench
and play his flat guitar? Polish
his greaves, cultivate his grapes?
And, ah yes, the Virgin. How did
the child not slip off her lap, he
thought. Some clay from Eden's
riverbank must have stuck him there.

II.

You said that when she stood against
the light and then oblique to it
she vanished and the other one,
the young one with the peaked brows,
how he too, astride the light,
slanted into it and you could not
tell, you said you could not tell,
exactly what he was or had been or
was it she who was so thin
that it became impossible to hook
them back for the shoot, she in her
linen cut on the bias, he in a blouse
of bruised silk, both shod in python or was it kid?

It is a long haul to the runway
bringing up the flesh and bone,
all tied together with sensual
hoods and belts. But the Holy Ghost
(and you did insist on this)
on a fling through time, smiled
at them the sudden smile
of those just brutally resurrected.

Proust Dying

He lay tumescent on the horns of paradise.
Through the curvature of the bedposts
he saw the tribe moving from portal
to portal through cascades of silk, upon
the skintight soul toward corridors
of sex, where all the stammering world
stood still. He peered round the
footman's buttocks and saw God
take tea with the doorman at the Ritz.

The Sleeping Lifeguard

He dreams of windows that flutter
open into eddies of sunlight
and fillets of spume. I came
round on the twentieth lap
and he lay perfectly asleep
as the waves slammed against
the world's cool belly. He
stirred in his slumber and plunged
through the water to the rock
bed beneath all waters
that reach back into the Eden
waters, those thorns
of tempest that compelled
the whirlpools and fleets
and the babble of sperm to speak dominion.

I Have Thoughts about the Density of Mountains

I have thoughts about the density of mountains.
Could there be at the center magnetic pebbles,
clusters of nuclear seeds, slivers of raw light,
and axle, spoke, rim of God's distracted
speculation on the circle? If I cut through to
the center, what scents and colors might my
knife push up, the blade washed with the flush
of thunder, curled like fronds about foaming
plates of ore, shifting over darkness, devouring
the sun afloat, laboring, coursing with erotic
gloom, brooding on a body candled by stars
in their first exaltation? O how large is sex!
I have thoughts about the density of mountains
and how mountains are the body that will never be.
I think about women and their thoughts, moving
toward the culminant plain like turtles bellied
out from their carapace.

The Green Trumpet

There is a wooden floor in a castle in Prague
where a court followed a king around: his orb
and closed crown, his etched, immense rings,
and keys that hung from his belt, keys to the room
beyond the iridescent fans and cod pieces.
That night in rooms of mellifluous cabinets
and vats of cyanide alone he leaned on
the window sill where desire in his nest
brooded in the dark. He thought: the water
supply is dank with rot, the street pocked,
the war has left the corpses like blighted
sheaves of wheat in the marketplace.
But desire still, there beyond that window,
pushed up against him, forcing him off balance
and onto the floor, the keys clattering against
him and the green trumpet, ice green, broke
from its throat a dark note, an atrocity,
barren of pitch, blowzy, a ludic bellow.

The Sound of the Launching
of a Thousand Ships

Her eyes did it, not her thighs or
breasts like ingots of clay. No question.
Paris had laid them all, every mortal,
wench, every goddess in her soubrettes
of halos and the odd boy on his
breezy ass, but only Helen could launch
a ship. By looking at the keel
or bow or mast, she could set them
quivering as she did Paris cock.
No, it was only she who could unhitch
the fleet from dry dock and send them
scuttling down into the water
that received them and pointed them toward the slaughter.

The Mount Athos Poems

You stung me with your flesh
and bold eyes in this scorched
sapphire and crushed salt light
where there is thunder in the
honeycomb, in the incense
and tinkling bells. I
harrowed my soul there like
the wild boars, scavengers of
the debris cast over them at
midnight of watermelon rinds
and stale bread. O this sensual
parade, this fatiguing palace,
where ikons and dreams of octopus
and olive oil have settled into
nests of gold, in the belly's
stupor amid drones of hexagons.

To be unclothed and on
another's flesh? But watch
your sensual speech as the
tides bring you to the
cascading shore and wine
all gone to sand. Trust never,
never the drift of eyes
or the colloquy of lips
untethered, when all is aloft,
or find yourself moored
on a mud flat, your poor
mind caught in a syrup of levers.

II.

The mind can become disjointed
as the bones in the neck
brought up and apart from the shoulders
and this did it. A vat of well water
from torrents high on the holy mountain
where snow in mid-summer hangs
in crevices like scorched salt
and submerged in it
a silver net that holds
raw venom from a killer snake: drunk
after the fangs had snared the blood
it wards off death. But when bone
and muscle coiled round and round
and round and the glands of the beast
pushed through my skin I could not reach
the vat in time to stop the locked
breath, the stanched breath, the
suffocating spiral before
the stricken, final, conduct of languor.

III.

Two men lay
naked on this
parterre and beneath
them on the surface
of shale and mica
seed streaks up
to disturb their
rest.

What shall I do
one cried to the
other, what shall
I ever do?

——

Do nothing.
Be still.
Let us be still.

But I cannot
the other said
I am too full
of this long day
and its intolerable
shades and scans
of light. I would
move on and go
beyond it.

Do not. Let us
lie here. Feel the earth
beneath,
the wings of the birds,
sharp mica,
the seeds' voluptuary
hum.

I feel the cover
of frost, the other said.

But sleep clamped
their eyes shut
and desire, downwind
like a hawk
circling the grazing lamb
swerved toward these two
stunned accomplices
in that deft
preludium before
their final trek up country.

The Building that the Body Is

The building that the body is
is combed with crofts and hinged
traps and below the wetlands
in the clamped-down soul
clamoring.

The building that the body is
in the house of the heart, surveyed, blind-walled
and there are coops there, coops of bandits
in the clamped-down blood
scampering.

The building sex is, in
the house of the heart and in the building
the body is: no pillar, no guardian wind,
no beam but all tumbling
in gravel wind, gravel wind. . . .

The Rainbow

You mistake the rainbow for
it is not it but a cross
section of the heart that
has been split by the hot
cormorant bird desire. Italian
bird, the stuttering barque,
the golden splutter.

Whew!

Long before the start of it
I heard the scud of love
across the heart. I heard
it in the sunlight real
as vine, in the charged
duplicity of the streets,
in discord (flies in
carnivorous drone on a
plate of crusts and grease).
On every common thing:
a geranium, a fountain—
planted bullets, even as
doors open from fine barns.

Three Poems for Nicos Stravroulakis

NAKED

I have this to say
about the unclothing of the clothed:
becoming naked is a turnabout
of what is ordered and decreed:
we are told to hide the flesh,
to hitch it to a stitch
or hem: lacking belt, buttons,
trousers and cap the luminous
layer of skin would increase
in splendido and corruscation
and be itself a vestment
and a peak of voluptuousness
and the elephantine seeds
of desire would grow up round
like vines of flame and
the coiled daysprings about
the heart would spin from the
ribcage and be imperial and unappeased
aroused beyond the shipwreck's flat clarion bells.

GATEAU AU MIEL

No. Exactly no. Yet
at the same moment
he leaned against
a wall. My mind
folded and unfolded
down the regions
of nakedness to the vanishing
point. There was never
a saint who doubted

it: the gnawing
at the ribbons in the breviary,
the wobble in the iridescent
alleluias, the ripe peach
through the candlelight and musk
in the mirrors of incense.

THE MOON VIEWING PLATFORM SEEN FROM THE SECOND ROOM OF THE OLD SHOIN KATURA

In, toward this unscanned
light, I stand on my wooden
viewing box to see
the moon. The land there is still
as dough. Flocks of shadow lean
on me for no soul's attached
and ladders of silence and loose bone
and desire uncalipered
prowl toward this keen iota of distance.

Too Hot, Too Hot

I would like to climb with you
the Scala Contarini
in the Corte dal Volvolo and tell you
that Hippasus drowned
when he revealed the existence
of the incommensurables.
Or we could think about
the Apocatastasis
when everything will be restored
even to the lost button
on your sleeve
or ask you if the Sensus Quadruplex
was your premier grand cru.
I want to know about
your virtuosity,
the melody of your life
that you cast
over my skin
like a runaway forge.
Do you believe
that a portion
of everything is in
everything? Anaxagoras of Clazomenae
did.

O je cris
donc je suis:
je chante
donc je gourverne.

Let us run naked to the tomb
of Patroclus
to find "that beauty which
makes us despair."

An Ecstasy: Bernini in Mind

I saw beneath the veil of sheet
a body's form I knew: exact as
keys and cups: the cupboard of a body:
knives, spoons, the marketplace,
the fleshly chattel. In a contraption
of frost, in a cowl of stopped waters
I hung above it, a satyr in breach
of dream, naked, coal-black goatee
and ruby bat. In its lewd ascension
of flesh, the sheet pulled back
and I fell akimbo on its languid chest
in a torrent of restoration, in a festal cannonade.

Dreams Erotic, Dreams Not

The sheet was pulled tight
across, each corner snapped
in a steel crease. The light
bounced on the pasty
afternoon and drenched the ceiling.
It was a theological dream.
Each perceptible languor
each conciliatory bark
each visitation
was implied in the sheet
and its contour
like a desert
with a bowl of fire at the center.
The going was rough:
back and forth
or simply incontestable balking.

Love

I shall remember your scarf
twisted around your head like a leaf
around a flower
in the bole of spring,
a stunted thing,
never to bloom,
a speaking frost.
And the light on your neck,
my shadow on your spine,
your belly like a moon.
I was enclosed by you
to the absolute severing of all light.
You opened your arms
and took me like
yarn to the wheel.
I would have climbed you like a ladder.
I have placed upon this sheet
the lumber of desire.
When you lie down, your spine so,
aligned along the crease
I shall thrum your bones to sing.

After Birth

Everything scattered, scattered everywhere.
Scattered. Everything. Everywhere. So
observed. Nothing did remain but untethered,
restored to the instant fragment,
groaning, pushing against the day's
weighted contour. The whole shuddering
and the window raised up and beyond
the green of the leafed sun, the apple
tree, the slow light. I thought how
it was never again to be possible to be
the same as I was before everything was
scattered everywhere and the crosshatch
and woven rushes burst and the smell of
afterbirth cascading down over my eyes
ending it all. Again.

These Tumultuous, These Erratic, These Crazy Waters

These tumultuous, these erratic, these
crazy waters. A fat lady turned
the corner and I thought of Titus
Andronicus and how life could never
be like that and yet I knew it was.
I was always within his sight:
a twist in a rope:
a furrow off target for the cast
bowl of seed and the skein of
darkness as it overtook his eyes.
Life is a thin membrane of ice,
the ceiling a tracery of upended
glacial leaves. We heard
the streams of spring rush beneath
the cover of frost. Oh to be caught
in a quest without end, in a calamity
of wrong turns, a wheel off the axle
spinning downhill toward the obsidian
wall where all ruckus had gone
to petrifaction.

When I Had Thought of Fire

When I had thought of fire I thought
of berries in the moss. I did not think
of furnaces. When I was a child fate
was in my hands, leaping from one rock
to another, scraping off my skin like
shelved cups cracked. I had eyes for
the luminous portals—waterfalls, the
ecstatic baldachin rising up from the
glazed munificence of air: the grove
of maples where I dragged Man Mountain Dean
when I found him dead in his stall, his
mane, slivers of frost, his great hoofs
frozen in dung, his eyes open unto the moors
of galloping spring and the cacophony of the reined-in heart.

Expenses

It cost exactly that—
no more, no less
than he had thought
it would. He added
the column on the left,
then on the right
and found they came out
on the balance exact
and when the sums were
subtracted from the
catastrophic final
agony he was aghast
and saw about him the
graphs of desolation,
pure and staggering.
The gods hulked against
the blue hills, their eyes
pierced by love. They
thought he had paid too much
for passion and the currents
of judgment swelled his
heart. He cast himself
into the whirlwind where he
had once been on an outing.

A Spiritual Experience

Handel's sister fainted when she
heard a chord Beethoven wrote; her
soul brushed against a hedgehog, her cheek-
bone shook. It was just too much
all round, nothing like her brother's
scaletta of tone sliding through
the eardrums.

A nun went to market. "I fear
an assault." Her prickly soul
contorted on the tarmac. Riding
on the hood she saw God, who
tipped his millennium cap
and pointed to the steam pushing
from the engine.

The nun, whose mission had been
salad for the evening meal, fell
dead upon the wheel, crashed a
road divider, plunged into a field
and lay open to the broaching fire wheels.

Desire

Di mi se mai fu fatta alcuna cosa?
—
E so ben ch'i' vo dietro a quel che m'arde.

I.

Have you heard that in the dust of India
zero rose from the dervish sands
or that God speaks to the tamarind tree?
I know we are never finished with unknowing.

II.

The way thought then was
through the long hall
in the Victoria and Albert:
a crucifixion of Pisano
(ivory with tints of color)
a four- or five-inch
Michelangelo of a dying nude
(or had he just fallen asleep?)
a wood French angel
with mouth agape and a broken
knight on his sarcophagus, himself
his tomb and oh yes that ivory
Byzantine Virgin in the round
and desire in its salty lassitude,
its flamboyant mouth
seen through the crenelations of its
cage, ruinous space, calling,
calling out through altitudes of light
sweeping into the Pleiades
where God, his scarf spinning,
behind him, stalks through space.

III. FRAGMENTS OF A
SONNET TO NO ONE

When you stood that morning
by the door wrapped
in a towel, your face wet
from a shower,
hair flat upon your nipples
I think that had I
pulled the cloth
away and had seen your body
head to toe
we might have known
the sensuous favor of the gods.
You are a memory in a field,
a creature moving through
the meadows, a pelt of shadow,
an obscure beneficence,
an infleshed lamentation.

If there be nothing to be said
but that it cannot be, then stop
the light that touches your
eyes, cover your neck. Raze them.
In memory's interference I have
turned to stone, under the rain
of that volcanic dust
you utter when you speak.

I would have summoned
from the scarves and tissue
of the light, your flesh, but
rapture stalled and the common
forms of love I could not
consecrate. No live thing

will tarry long with me. The memory
of desolation marks me like
an hex and when I touch a
body it recoils and leaves me
as if the love-demons dwelt within my blood.

Swans in the Dark

The rain so thick, the dark was clotted by it.
Passage through it, constricted in the waters,
made tumid by it, blinded me. I steered through
it, flayed by the fall of the cloth of wind,
bark of some celestial oak whipped round to
a silken whip. "Watch for the darkness rising up,"
he called. I held a torch to the surface,
away from my eyes. He shouted, "Catch any
darkness rising up out of the dark. It's
bound to be a rock." I thought of a body that
rose up once out of the dark that closed
the dark again with darkness. Then across
the runnel of light I saw two swans bearing
down upon the bow, two pure beeswax candles
unlit in the channels that run crossways
over my heart's packed-down tumultuous glacier.

Rounding It Out, Paring Down, Letting Go

For Jane Mayhall

A way of seeing:
The acceptance of the lawn
and the wall at the end of it,
a door in the wall to another
lawn and door: emptiness: to inhabit
emptiness is not the poet's
labor but glory rather,
then the interference of children,
the pots and pans, the husband
and accumulated shoes and door
into parlors and rows
of tulips and daffodils in pots
arranged and then arranged again
so they turn to the sun in its
perch beyond burning: the manipulation
of the sun to get it right where
one commands it go—or the flesh
in the imprecision of it or the precision
of it at full gallop but not it
nor lawns or doors are
the calibrations of the poet. To that end
one sure thing: the jaguars move on
and the dolphins just cover their eyes.

Les situations nettes

THE WILTING NARCISSUS AND TULIPS

Tomorrow they will have turned
blue, a ceremonial tinge, funereal,
to be scattered beside your bedside
O cool betrothed, unaccustomed
to delight. You are a mortal folly.
The blossoms descend toward the tabletop
till they are flat upon it, like palls.

A DARE

My consort now, once again, language:
ferocity of words, now, once again
tied to my soul and flesh, down, like
speared Grecian hip or the clipped-off,
full-blown sumptuous rose. I am there
again at the words' first gasp into
shape: the "guh" of God, the "tr" of tree,
the "ca" of color, the "eh" of is: its entirety.

BODY 1

Let down the window,
pull up the rugs,
repaint the walls,
cast out the chipped vase,
paint it all a moss yellow.
Find a new mirror.
Simplify the gallery so
that it seems an alley of yew.
Your body comes
upon itself

as the sun clamps down
on the bed
and there is nothing
beside you but
the tinged air
having come but just then
from the window without curtains
and found you cold as herbs
round a stone.

BODY 2

What? What is it? Some plainsong
out of lust? A calendar unfolding?
Long shadows out of sorrow? I
speculate on this with conviction
that too late I've lived without
abandonment. Never, never has the body
in discontent so fierce it could not stand
erect, concluded argument and stripped,
elected mortal ruination and gone
catapulting through the air that lies
between the lips and the atonal groin.

BODY 3

Back then, to the beginning
where the great tent was and sand
and wind and the bray of hounds,
where Father willed the death of his
son and where the scorn of his
dicta and contra dicta caused
a mark to form on my thigh, a blooded
wave that was for a lover the sign of a desert.

BODY 4

It contains what it is not
and it is what it contains.
It must die, yet what it
contains dies not. What dies
does not but curls round worms
and nourishes vines. What it
contains and what it contains not,
in some jolt of the aethers and globe
will come again like those in
a promenade, reaching a triumphant
turn in the road see the horizon
filled with sails and freshets of thunder.

BODY 5

Listen: the torrent
lifts its tongue
to the roof of ice
and I hear your heart
beat: it rushes onto the dam
where the mill is, frozen
to the millstone.
I feel the coil spring
at the juncture wherein you
join all directions in stunned accord.

BODY 6

Against the snow: against the snow
in a blue contraption of wings
and ribs crossed over in a release
of uncoiled light I watch the body
as it watches the blue body and its contraption
head onward to the blue aphrodisiacs.

BODY 7

When I throw the sheets back
and cup cold water in my hands
to douse my head, and I step
from my body sealed fast to my ribs
by the night's calking,
I lean on the sill
and look out over the land,
lying like a platter of fresh-cropped figs
on the steaming fields of the musky light.

BODY 8

The six-inch high marble torso
of crucified Christ with polychrome
black hair, slightly waved to the shoulders,
and crown of thorn set round the skull,
rib cage delineated and belly's slope
like Golgotha, head dead weight
and neck stretched, reposed in ivory,
utterly corporeal yet stiff,
the soul, a rod poking through the flesh
rising with flared out groaning
capitulation toward the azure enthronement.

Aber wozu dann dies komplizierte ding?

Wittgenstein

"But what then is
the point of the
complicated thing?"
I have been given
a stranger nerve
and tendons
that carry
sweeps of terror
through me
to a gland
where the fool gods
made me quarry
to the heart's solemnities
folded like pins in my flesh.
For as I drove
to an island
where I'd been given haven
I passed a village
and could not go
beyond it
and swerved off in the sun
and glare,
my body and its acrobatic
breath
contorted like wrens
accosted
by a whirlwind.
I stood,

my hands locked together
and thought of ways
death might come: an aboriginal
wave, a refusal
of light, a freezing shadow.
This morning I
walked to a small cliff
gnawed
by the sea
to slate ravines and pools
of shells and weed
where lichen
and disemboweled
hunks of sea urchin
lay on
the copper field
of the bay.
On the sun's nape
I laid my hands
and felt
my skin shift
its hold on gravity
letting down
upon me
a chaplet
of lupin
and endless waters
that can
complete nothing
but render
stable
the infinite mountains
that rise up beneath
the wake of the swans.

Dark Secrets, Erotic Words and Glances

Hath stored from the beginning
the spies and counter-worlds
within the foot, at the instep's
arch, the trampoline that sends
us up into the air, searching
the castigations and the bountiful.
The dancer falls across
the path like a sheet lifted up
from the sleeping body and rams
the eyes. The brain touches the skull's crust.
Hath beside me for the days on end,
my soul, stirring like a bird trapped
in a tese, under the compulsion
of skin. The arm flashes signaling
shipwreck. My neck pulls across
my shoulder looking for the on-
coming. This is the terminus
of dark secrets, glances, of
the erotic message, the semaphore
out beyond the skin.
Hath increased now beyond dams and
locks to this escarpment, to this
fastness. To this catastrophe
I have brought no skill to end
or to begin an ending: just
the on and on of it, unfinished
from da capo to an impulsion and
the air, the melody undone
toward me to encompass all, to
redeem this boisterous invention.

Hath increased this inundation
I cannot stem nor turn back,
reverse, restore to clay. I am
anointed, the orb in hand, the oils
pressed into my brow, the hood of devastation
on my head, the mortal things
incumbered for flesh's duration with
you who hath contained since the beginning, me.

The Five Seasons of Obsession

I have not, by your instruction, Lord,
learned a rubric of obsession
that will get me out of its crack
and crooning. A cataclysmic drone
of it all day is a hindrance
to thinking and I would be rid of it.

Perhaps it is a fault in the ceding
of the genetic currents.
The galleon sighted, the school
of cool gray fish floating
through the tired waters, late
in summer, a brazier of tulips lit

by their stems—anything will do
it: pushed-over rake and shovel,
a cat behind a bush of laurier roses,
two children on a seesaw, scissors
on a table, blades open, the spine
of a book, a patch of sand hit

by a wave. The four seasons of obsession
come quick, go, return again, repeat,
mirror it all so that it soon becomes
a feast I no longer unearth the
flacons of wine nor fire the cannon
for. On the stoop I sit

to await the fifth season
when the coded sun, the trickle of blood,
the fissure in my cranium, the

whole assembled platoon of obsession
will face the east wind and in
amazed precision unravel Him whose

mien is the resolution of all contrariness.